MW00996049

PRAISE

HOW MUCH LONGER

This book is witty and relatable, and for goodness sake, somebody should make a TV show out of this family. I'm a super fan and would watch all 21 seasons.

— MISSY SHIRLEY, AUTHOR, *ALL THE LIES SHE TOLD* & *STORYBOOK LAKE* SERIES

Is there room for one more at the Thanksgiving table? These stories leave me hoping the kids will adopt me as their favorite aunt so I, too, can be part of the Earnheardt's big life."

— BONNIE JEAN FELDKAMP, SYNDICATED COLUMNIST, OPINION EDITOR FOR *THE LOUISVILLE COURIER JOURNAL*

The Earnheardt family account of their family life during the quarantine is relatable but also uplifting. The stories remind you how the small family moments are the real milestones.

— REBECCA REGNIER, JOURNALIST, HUMOR COLUMNIST, AUTHOR OF THE *WIDOW'S BAY* SERIES

Adam and Mary Beth's book reads like a classic TV sit-com about a typical American family enduring life's challenges. More importantly, it offers a wonderful message about the power of a family's shared love and the value of creativity, especially in tougher times.

— DAVE LIEBER, COLUMNIST, *THE DALLAS MORNING NEWS*

Every young family needs to read (and chuckle while reading) the Earnheardt Family collection of reflections, HOW MUCH LONGER. Mom and Dad (extremely talented writers with a grand sense of humor) and the energetic Earnheardt kids chronicle the pandemic experience from their house to ours.

— JIM TRESSEL, PAST PRESIDENT, YOUNGSTOWN STATE UNIVERSITY AND COLLEGE FOOTBALL FALL OF FAME INDUCTEE

Adam and Mary Beth are first rate chroniclers of the pandemic's impact on ordinary middle-class life. Consequently, there's enough humor mixed with honest observations about their family's daily challenges to show us all how to survive and emerge from profoundly unfunny times with our empathy and love for life mostly intact.

— TONY NORMAN, COLUMNIST, NEXTPITTSBURGH AND CHAIR, INTERNATIONAL FREE EXPRESSION PROJECT

HOW MUCH LONGER
ONE FAMILY'S JOURNEY THROUGH TWO YEARS OF HELL, HEALING, AND HILARITY

DR. ADAM C. EARNHEARDT

DR. MARY BETH EARNHEARDT

FOREWORD

Mark Sweetwood,
former editor of *Mahoning Matters*

The story of how the Earnheardts became "The Earnheardts," and now "How Much Longer," takes a little explanation.

Within five months of the launch of the *Mahoning Matters* digital news site, the staff faced a crisis. In our first five months, nearly every day sparked a crisis for our fledgling operation. We had launched Oct. 9, 2019, just 40 days after the closure of Youngstown, Ohio's daily newspaper, *The Vindicator*.

The goal of what was then called the Compass Experiment was to cultivate and create new media ecosystems in the era of newsroom cutbacks and closures across the globe. In the United States, Google had partnered with McClatchy, then a family-run newspaper chain, for the effort. Mandy Jenkins was hired as general manager and the Ohio native thought the Youngstown situation — a combination of a high-profile closure and a plethora of connected journalists now seeking work — would make a good spot for the first of three U.S. Compass communities.

She hired two amazing Vindicator reporters — Justin Dennis and Jess Hardin — and then me, the former Vindicator managing editor. We cajoled long-time Vindy copy editor Jeremy Harper to the team as well as former Vindicator ad sales representative Mark Eckert. And as we worked to develop major news pieces to distinguish *Mahoning Matters* from the local pack of news entities, COVID-19 creeped in and stopped the world in March 2020.

Everything closed. Public meetings stopped. Businesses were shuttered. Access to city hall to file record requests? Nope. In person meet-and-greets like the "Pitch Nights" we were making famous? Done. Long-form interviews for deeper stories? Nobody was at work or even cared to return calls.

To a young news team, COVID-19 seemed kind of personal since it undermined us at every turn. Then it turned very personal, when Mark became one of the first Mahoning County victims. His death sent us reeling.

As we pivoted to figure out what *Mahoning Matters* should be in this new world, our audience began to tell us. We could watch analytics and see which stories were resonating. And readers began to call and email us: What is this virus? What stores deliver? What restaurants do curbside delivery? Can a business force me to wear masks? What kinds of tests are the best? And, eventually, where can I get vaccinated?

People were asking us to help them cope. Our content switched from deep dives to utility journalism to answer the call. Less long-form narrative stories and more lists. And I reached out to the community for columnists. A lawyer to answer questions. A minister to nourish our damaged spiritual psyches. And, a family that was unafraid to share the ups and downs of these complicated times.

Enter "The Earnheardts."

To be truthful, I was after Adam and Mary Beth Earnheardt for some time to contribute to *Mahoning Matters*. They represent the crossroads of journalism in the Mahoning Valley. Adam is professor in the Department of Communication at Youngstown State University and special assistant to YSU's provost. Mary Beth is professor of journalism in the same Department and the long-time faculty media advisor to YSU's student newspaper, *The Jambar*.

And, in full disclosure, both were kind of my bosses in my side gig as adjunct professor at YSU where I taught journalism and magazine writing.

Adam had contributed to many area news sites in columns that focused on parenting through emerging and social media. I was making a big ask: To look inward and share a family's struggles during a full-blown pandemic. And that also meant sharing the spotlight — uncomfortable as it might be at times — with their kids: Ella, Katie, Sadie, and Ozzie.

In late March, their first column arrived and I still remember reading it and being thrilled with that rare — for the pandemic era — slice of humanity: "Going to work and school can be stressful, but we also use those places as a sort of escape. Now, we were all working from home. At least in *Lord of the Flies*, no one was trying to video conference with colleagues on Zoom while a 7-year-old tried to ride the dog like a bull, the 9-year-old ate Froot Loops off the floor, and the 14-year-old and 12-year-old were sleeping in until noon after an all-nighter of Minecrafting."

I knew this would resonate with readers who were wondering about how other families were coping. What I didn't expect was for folks like my parents down in Florida to be as eager to read the weekly exploits of The Earnheardts as I was.

The Earnheardts helped me and countless others navigate the unexpected times we found ourselves in from 2020 to 2022. I'm forever grateful for their contributions and their friendship. What higher praise can there be other than: "You made a difference."

And now I'm privileged to introduce — both to readers familiar with those columns and to new folks who are about to discover their pandemic wisdom — this volume of the collected adventures of The Earnheardts.

1

HOW WE 'FAMILY' IN A PANDEMIC

ADAM & MARY BETH

School breaks are some of the best times for our family. Sure, they're a lot of work, but we look forward to spending time together as a family.

The big school breaks for parents like us come in winter and spring. We cherish the concerts, dinners, and other events that make up our holiday traditions, but seasoned parents go into these times with the reassuring thought that, when the break ends, our little ones are heading back to school.

We know that after a brief respite at home, we all go back to normal life. Parents head back to work. Children return to school to spend their days under the watchful eyes of dedicated teachers. Life returns to normal.

As a Midwestern family, we know there's a chance for a surprise snow day. We're Ohioans. We can handle it.

The problem with a pandemic and the resulting order to stay at home, however, was that we weren't really prepared to live like that. The "break" model we were used to was carefree, with lots of out-of-home options to distract us. We could escape. Now we were trapped with many more responsibilities than a normal break required. We were now our kids' teachers and entertainers, along with the traditional caretakers and disciplinarians.

We did some of these jobs part-time all along. Now we were full-time.

We were mentally and physically unprepared as parents to spend that much time together as a family, as were our four children. We used to think we were pretty good at the whole parenting thing. Now we were forced to face the fact that we may, in fact, be kind of bad at it. We needed to get better at it, and fast.

Adam likes to post funny little family conversations on his social media accounts. He starts each post with "Overheard at the Earnheardts". The day we found out the kids were going to have remote schooling for at least the next three weeks, he posted, "Think two weeks over Christmas and New Years is rough? It's about to get all *Lord of the Flies* up in here."

For those unfamiliar with *Lord of the Flies*, it's a reference to William Golding's book about a group of boys shipwrecked on a deserted island. They attempt to govern themselves with particularly horrific results.

It was a funny little one-off meant to reflect the chaos we anticipated. The truth is, it won't be *Lord of the Flies*, because our kids wouldn't be left to fend for themselves. Well, at least we hoped not. *Lord of the Flies* is a fantasy. Getting stranded with four kids on a locked-down, shelter-in-place island is a reality. Luckily, we have more than one floor in our home, something that feels only slightly larger than a studio apartment when it's filled with kids and dogs and a cat.

Going to work and school can be stressful, but we also use those places as a sort of escape. Now, we were all working from home. At least in *Lord of the Flies*, no one was trying to video conference with colleagues on Zoom while a 7-year-old tried to ride the dog like a bull, the 9-year-old ate Froot Loops off the floor, and the 14-year-old and 12-year-old were sleeping in until noon after an all-nighter of Minecrafting.

In spite of these challenges, we were starting to see some positive developments. We'd never heard our kids laugh together this much. Dinner time used to be a rushed event so that we could get to all the evening chores and still find time to drive the kids to dance and music and art lessons. Parenting used to be a constant negotiation about who-takes-or-picks-up-which-kid-from-which-thing. Now we were spending more time at the dinner table. We built 1000-piece puzzles. The kids taught Adam how to play Minecraft. We sat around and told stories. We talked about things like financial literacy and Elon Musk and digging tunnels to the center of the Earth. We learned to work as a team and be respectful of each other's needs—including needs for time and space.

Our busy lives took a pandemic pause, but this meant we were more present than ever in each other's lives, and we kind of liked it. We also understood that these were probably the early days of being together all day, and that the real struggle was ahead, with no promised end date in sight. No date to return to school was circled on the calendar. The real struggle would be maintaining our sanity when repetition stifled our creativity. The real struggle, we thought, would be patience when we're stuck in the same space together for weeks, possibly months, and beyond.

It's not perfect. No family is. No home is. Clearly, pandemic parenting perfection is a fool's errand. But as long as we give up on the idea that we were going to be the best parents ever and just take each day at a time, there was an opportunity to make some new magic in the lives of our children, and lots of lasting memories along the way.

2

RITES OF PASSAGE
MARY BETH & ADAM

There are several rites of passage for Earnheardt children.
It's likely you have similar transitional moments in your family. Things like big birthdays, learning to ride a bike, or graduating.

Some milestones are big. Others are smaller but serve as transitions that signify maturity. For example, turn 5 and you're off to kindergarten, probably with the first-ever school bus ride. Turn 15-and-a-half and you're eligible to get a driver's permit in our state, accompanied by free lessons from Dad.

Others have earned their place in Earnheardt family lore, in part because they're extra special, but also because the older kids have been talking to the younger kids about these events for years. For example, when an Earnheardt kid turns 6, they get to go to their first Pittsburgh Steelers game with Dad.

Yes, we get why that might not be appealing to some. Maybe you don't like sports or football, or you really hate the Steelers; we get it. But this was more than just about sports and football. One reason why we chose this special event was that it allowed us to teach our kids about fandom and community, about our extended family's passion for Pittsburgh sports, and the love we have for the region where we grew up. That's something most parents can appreciate, sports fan or not.

The other reason we chose it is because Adam needs more people willing to attend Steelers games with him — so he's intent on making at least one of our kids a lifelong member of Steelers Nation. Unfortunately, this rite of passage didn't really take. Most of our kids are not football fans, and so they'll likely only go back to Heinz Field because Dad promises bottomless cups of hot chocolate, popcorn, and a Primanti Brothers sandwich.

At age 8, another Earnheardt rite is the right to chew gum. This is a much-anticipated moment for the kids who dream of sampling different gum flavors and blowing the perfect bubbles. It's celebrated with all the Bubble Yum you can chew. Mary Beth stocks up on all sorts of flavors in the week leading up to an 8th birthday.

Maybe it's because we let him start a little bit early, but chewing gum didn't really "stick" with Oscar. Pun partially intended. "Meh," he said, after his first piece. "I don't get all the excitement. I'll stick with my Jolly Ranchers, thank you very much." Fast-forward to age 10 and he goes through more gum than all three girls combined. He loves the stuff.

But it's at age 11 that an Earnheardt kid experiences the most anticipated, glorious milestone of all, much more important than the Steelers game, bubble gum, or a big birthday. In fact, when Katie turned 10, she said with a sigh, "I'm just trying to get through this next year, so I can finally be 11."

This is because, at age 11, Earnheardt kids get their first smartphone.

When Sadie turned 11, a new smartphone was bestowed upon her, as if being crowned or knighted with a certain kind of power and great responsibility. Although we've been through this twice now with Ella and Katie, there was an added level of excitement with Sadie's smartphone celebration. Sadie is our social butterfly and, to hear her tell it, she has been "literally dying" without this particular accessory.

It's clear to us that her already-heightened sense of excitement had been amplified by the pandemic. When she was younger, a smartphone represented being grown. During the pandemic, it represented the sort of connectedness we were all hungry for. Unlike her older sisters, we didn't wait to prepopulate her phone with contact names and numbers of close family members. In fact, we even asked our family to text her "happy birthday" greetings so that when she powered it up for the first time, it would chime and vibrate to signal new messages and connections.

So, as we approached Sadie's birthday, all the kids were excited. Heck, Mom and Dad were excited, too. There was extra teasing and plans were made regarding apps and Spotify playlists and access to the Google Play family plan.

It might have been Sadie's big birthday, but for all Earnheardts, the end of April is madness. This is because it's a double birthday week. Katie turned 14 two days before Sadie's birthday. Before the pandemic, we'd try to cram them in between the million end-of-the-school-year activities, but now things were slower and we were ready to party. We ended up with a week-long celebration, not two distinct parties. Every day we wanted to do something special, like make a special cake, open presents, or call family and let them tell the kids happy birthday. It was a lot of fun.

Like most of the world, we were looking for reasons to move on, to transition away from death and disease and seemingly insurmountable odds. We wanted to leave the masks and Plexiglass behind and enjoy hanging out with friends in the fresh air. Many of us were looking for reasons to celebrate. We strived for change, but not just any change. We yearned for the kind of change that could propel our lives forward — and we wanted more than anything to bring our friends and family along with us, to celebrate with them, and to rekindle those dormant connections with humanity.

Even if our kids can't name it or give voice to it, we see them looking for this, too. They want reasons to go out and explore, to find new adventures. We see them looking for ways to make new connections, to find their friends online and in the real world, on their mobile devices, and at school.

It's been good to feel that sense of connection with them, and we certainly savored it during COVID. Like her big sisters, we felt like we were giving up a little piece of Sadie's innocence, of our baby girl, to an online world. She started telling us how she's feeling by sending us memes and emojis. Instead of coming to see us at night before she goes to sleep, she texts us. It's all part of growing up. We're just hoping that by creating these habits now, by providing her with different ways to connect, she'll never want to stop connecting with her parents and siblings.

Then, when she's a grown woman out on her own, hopefully she'll remember to take a few minutes to drop a big heart in the family group text.

3
PLANNING A (PAND)EPIC FAMILY VACATION
ADAM & MARY BETH

I n late 2020, there was a clear, albeit unspoken, understanding in our home that there would be no weekend trips this year. It's not that we're heavy travelers, but in normal times, we occasionally managed to take the kids to a local indoor water park, zoo, or some other outdoor extravaganza.

There are several reasons why we decided to forego these small adventures.

First, it wasn't safe. And even if we took the recommended precautions, it didn't sound like a very good time. I mean, who wants to sit poolside wearing a mask? No thanks. It just doesn't have the "rest and relaxation" vibe one would typically associate with a vacation.

Second, we had been worried about money. Yes, there were some outrageously good travel deals. Do a quick search of Vegas hotel deals in March 2021 to see what we mean. Even still, our budget, like that of many families, was much tighter than usual.

Finally, any family vacation we take next will be remembered for a lifetime. You might be thinking, "The Earnheardts must be doing it wrong. Aren't they all memorable?" Obviously, the answer would be yes. More of the time. Or maybe it's that all vacations are memorable in their own ways.

But this next vacation will be the first, big, post-pandemic (or, at least, hopefully, please-dear-God, near-the-end pandemic) family trip. At this point, we're all so desperate for new surroundings, that our next trip could be to outer Mongolia, and we'd be satisfied (all due respect to outer Mongolians).

Even in good times, we didn't have a huge travel budget, so we're not too hard to please. Our last epic family vacation was a trip to Niagara Falls in June 2019. Our kids like to say they "traveled abroad" because, well, if you really want to see the Falls, you've got to see them from both sides: U.S. and Canada. So, passports in hand, we crossed the border.

We did the typical touristy things on that trip. We rode the Maid of the Mist. We tasted Canadian maple syrup (sorry Canada; it tastes the same as the U.S. variety). We ate dinner at the world-famous Flying Saucer Restaurant. We watched amazing light shows and fire-works that lit up the nighttime sky and spray from the Falls. We successfully stopped Oscar from jumping the fence to, as he put it, "go for a swim." Adam even suggested that as a precautionary measure, Oscar should wear a life preserver when observing the Falls.

Memories of that last Earnheardt vacation seem so distant now. We have photos and videos, but the real memories are fading. We were craving something new, but mostly, we were looking for an escape. We wanted a release from the mundane life of going to work and school, coming home, making dinner, cleaning house, and doing homework, going to bed, and waking up to do it all over again – day after day – all while living under the COVID cloud.

We actually like being around each other, which is a feat for a family of six. But we thought we'd really like to be around each other a lot more in a different location for a few days.

We were also craving an escape from Youngstown, Ohio. Nothing against Youngstown or our Valley in northeast Ohio. We moved here specifically to raise our little family. We've been comforted by the way our community reacted to the pandemic. But as the pandemic lingered, so did our wanderlust.

When even the thought of a short weekend away wasn't in the cards, we did the next best thing: we wished, and we dreamed, and we planned.

Mary Beth read that one of the best parts of a vacation is planning it. She's right. It gives us something to look forward to. According to a study in *Applied Research in Quality of Life*, Jeroen Nawijn and his colleagues found that "Vacationers reported a higher degree of pre-trip happiness, compared to non-vacationers, possibly because they are anticipating their holiday."

Anyone who travels knows the fun in selecting the location, dates, hotel rooms, and (Adam's favorite part) all the places you'll eat.

That's exactly what we did — we thought about the next big epic family getaway. We talked about it for months, throwing out ideas on fun, but relatively inexpensive locations within driving distance (i.e., for us, that's about 8 hours these days). Earlier that year, our kids had provided some very elaborate vacation ideas.

We don't think we're ready for some of their suggestions just yet, but we've landed on a location. While we've been in the mood to plan a vacation, country music legend Dolly Parton had been in the news recently (don't worry, it was for good reasons — as if there would be a bad reason for Dolly to be in the news). Somehow those two things mixed and voila, we planned a late-summer trip to Dollywood.

Mary Beth had been advocating for this since well-before March 2020, but it took the pandemic for the stars to align. The kids drank her Kool-Aid — even if they (and Mary Beth) can only hum along to "9 to 5" — and the idea of going to an amusement park in the Great Smoky Mountains emerged as a good cure for cabin fever.

Adam, the family musicphile, planned to educate the family

about Dolly's music with a Spotify list on the long car ride to Pigeon Forge, Tennessee.

Normally, everyone would sit back and let Adam make the vacation decisions, but this time, we involved the kids more. They all wanted a hot tub. Sadie wanted her own bed. Ella wanted a pool. Oscar wanted to hug Dolly Parton. Katie wanted to catch a pigeon (see, she's got this thing for birds, and she thought that if we're going to a place called Pigeon Forge... oh, never mind).

We saw the anticipation grow when we talked and planned. We worked together to create something that we marked on the calendar and counted down the days. It was fun, but more importantly, it was hopeful – something that'd been dearly lacking during COVID.

We were likely to still need our masks, and there would probably be reduced capacities in the park (which might be a good thing: i.e., shorter ride lines!). But for the first time in a long time, we had a sense of optimism. As a family, we were looking ahead to taking a step out into the world, to let our minds grow and heal, to see something new together far away from the mundane and misery.

It was a tenuous start to the healing process, but it held, and our family enjoyed an epic experience. As COVID continues to wane, our family will be off on more epic adventures, making memories that will last a lifetime.

4

TAKE-OUT IS SURVIVAL

MARY BETH

I t's hard to prepare meals for a family of six. Even under the best circumstances, there are dissatisfied customers. In spite of the challenges, in pre-pandemic times, we rarely ate out. When we did, it was a treat for everyone. I didn't have to cook for a bunch of ingrates, Adam didn't have to clean the kitchen, and the children got to avoid my food.

When restaurants were forced to move to take-out-only at the start of the pandemic, the children pounced on the opportunity to order food from their favorite establishments. Suddenly, eating out was not merely a way to avoid vegetables, it was their civic duty.

Of course, they didn't come up with the "civic duty" argument on their own. Adam and I have instilled the importance of supporting local businesses and attending community events into their brains. As soon as they were old enough to comprehend the philosophy of giving back to the community, we started doing things to reinforce this idea. It's normal for us to take the kids Christmas shopping on Small Business Saturday, visit the downtown for festivals and events, and support our neighborhood.

Heck, we could dress a small army in all our Defend Youngstown gear – a line of merchandise developed by Youngstown community organizer, Phil Kidd.

As we face this national crisis, the philosophy of giving back is more important than ever. If we want to keep our friends' and neighbors' businesses afloat during the next few months, those of us who can need to pump money into our local economy.

Adam and I have both worked at bars and restaurants. I remember the stress of looking at the calendar to see how many hours I was scheduled to work the next week and the anxiety of trading shifts with co-workers. In those days, it was common for me to miss important events because of my work schedule, and, even when I was supposed to be off, there was always a chance of being called in at the last minute.

Most importantly, I remember how much I needed that money to survive.

For those who have never worked in the service industry, it's hard and unpredictable. I can't imagine how difficult and uncertain it is now. Even though it's been years since we worked in restaurants, Adam and I still feel solidarity with the wait staff. And because we respect them, it has been our common practice to opt for take-out rather than dine-in service. It may seem counterintuitive, but when the six of us head into the world, it's not good news for those working at our destination.

The Earnheardts are a bit of a nightmare, and sometimes a generous tip just isn't worth it. I imagine servers see us coming and choose straws to decide who will wait on our table. Before the pandemic, we tried to be normal restaurant patrons. We'd head out for a night on the town, always hopeful for an evening of family bonding. Adam would greet the host with a smile, and help the staff move tables together to accommodate our large family. In spite of our best intentions, most nights started with a battle of seating arrangements. The big kids fought hard to sit together, far away from the littles, while the littles tried to insert themselves between a parent and a hostile older sibling.

After we managed to get seated, there was usually a brief respite while the little kids did whatever activity was offered on a restaurant placement (coloring, tic-tac-toe, etc.). But as sure as I'm Youngstown proud, as soon as the little kids finished their coloring pages, the phone wars would start.

It's a digital divide between the bigs and the littles, the haves and the have-nots, the cell phone users and the jealous others. There's no winning resolution. If I forbade phones at the table, the big kids sulk. If I let the big kids use their phones, the little ones whine. No matter what we did, it didn't produce a happy environment for a family meal. As the meal progressed, so did the frustration. We'd spill drinks, drop food, and were way too loud. By the end of it, there was usually at least one of us crying into a to-go box, and those of us who weren't, wanted to.

Now that we've been home for three weeks, I would love to see my kids making each other miserable at our favorite neighborhood restaurants. Since that's not an option, we've been upping our take-out game. The shock is that we're much better at take-out than we were at dining out. Along the way, we've learned some useful tricks for feeding kids take-out.

First, we start planning for dinner at least two hours before mealtime. This allows enough leeway for fighting over the choice of take-out destinations, finding a menu, explaining different food options, and threatening to call the whole thing off.

Second, when in doubt, we order pizza. This is the only food you can safely assume will feed a lot of kids. The first time any parent is charged with feeding more than two kids a single meal, they suddenly understand that pizza is magic. You can feed adults pretty much anything because most fear being difficult. Grownups will either feign a lack of appetite or eat whatever nonsense you choose to serve. But kids won't play that game. At least one of them will act as a spoiler and reject what you serve. If you want a drama-free dinner, pizza night is a must.

Finally, eat out a lot and local. Protect your neighborhood during these difficult times. Tell the kids in your life about how hard people are working to keep them safe and well-fed. Tell them about the first responders and health care workers on the front lines of this virus, but don't forget about those who do the jobs we sometimes take for granted--delivery drivers, grocery store clerks, warehouse workers, and the scores of people in the Valley preparing our meals.

We look forward to the day when we can visit those restaurants in person again. We'll be overjoyed to sit at an extra-large table and make a mess and be loud and obnoxious. Until then, we'll hunker down, order food, and be thankful for those in our community who take care of us.

5

GEN X PARENTS: BUILT FOR A PANDEMIC

MARY BETH

I don't usually insert myself into generational warfare, but ever since my 12-year-old started responding to my orders with an eye roll and, "OK, Boomer," I've discovered a rage I didn't know existed. She uses it as a punchline, a rhetorical tool to get a reaction, but I receive it as a slur.

I'm not a Boomer. I'm also not a Millennial. I am a Gen Xer, and it's time the kids learn what my generation is capable of. We're often overlooked and most of us are okay with this because we like to keep to ourselves. The generational scholars can spend their time writing about Boomers and the Millennials, we don't care. We're not the silent generation, we're the "Don't bother us and we won't bother you" generation.

But now that it's pandemic time, social media has come alive with my people. In a strange turn of events, Gen X has something to say. We have advice for the masses. We are the generation that was built to shelter-in-place. If you learn to live like us, you'll be OK. We know this on a gut level, but there is also research to back it up. Even though we're not a favorite subject of study, in the instances where academics were forced to grapple with our existence, they kind of nailed it.

William Strauss and Neil Howe referred to Gen Xers as "nomads." They point to the fact that we were born during a cultural awakening, "a time of social ideals and spiritual agendas when youth-fired attacks break out against the established institutional order." If you know any Gen Xers, you've probably heard them talk about their flower-child, hippy parents who marched to protest war, experimented with drugs, and "loved" everyone. This was great for our parents, but all their freedom left them little time to attend to our needs.

The research describes nomads as under-supervised, slightly unprotected children. We came into this world as an alienated group, but we grew into responsible young adults, often leading frenetic, exhausting lives. Here's the catch that makes us perfect for the current moment: nomads are also pragmatic midlife leaders during a crisis who will age into resilient post-crisis elders.

This certainly rings of truth. The average Gen X childhood was much different than what we see today. It's not that our parents weren't around, they just did distinctly adult things while we were left to fend for ourselves. I grew up on a farm, so my experience was a little bit different, but I saw how my friends lived.

When I would get off the bus with one of them (which was often), we were left on our own until the parents arrived. Sometimes there would be an older sibling around, absent-mindedly guarding the ship. For the most part, we had the run of whatever house we invaded. When we got home from school, we'd eat cereal or ramen, and watch lots of television.

My husband Adam is also a Gen Xer. He grew up just north of Pittsburgh, and although he's a city boy and I'm a country girl, our loosely-supervised childhood experiences are very similar. Now we're drawing on the strength we gained from our misspent youth to help our kids through the lockdown.

We know firsthand just how resilient children can be. We're cool with the kids scrounging the kitchen for chips and pop (it was good enough for us). We love to hear complaints about boredom (try being alone for hours with no internet, then we'll talk). If the kids are going to grow into their potential, it's our duty to let them alone so they can teach themselves how to play a guitar or code a video game. In our experience, being parented is the real drag on a child's creative genius.

When we were little, even when our parents came home from work, they didn't play with us or ask us how the day went. They were too tired for that nonsense. So we'd do our homework, do the dishes, and either hit the streets, explore the woods, or isolate in our rooms where we'd listen to local radio, create mixtapes, and sing into our hairbrushes.

Think about it: if there was ever a time to make a mixtape, it's now.

We used sharpies to draw on our ripped jeans and create our own tie-dyed shirts. We built forts from blankets and living room furniture. We made collages from Tiger Beat magazine cut-outs while our siblings had cardboard lightsaber duels. We are capable of having fun while being socially isolated because it reminds us of the good old days.

We survived by finding things in our environment and using them for creative play. If we made it through childhood (yes, the lack of supervision had some consequences), it was off to college where we continued to cultivate useful pandemic behaviors.

Our fashions were focused on comfort. Even when we went out, Gen Xers wore flannel shirts, combat boots, and baby doll dresses. I don't miss my work clothes. I'm teaching my kids the freedom of grunge.

After we flatten the curve and start to move about the world again, it'll be time to tackle the collapse of the economy. It's a good thing college prepared us for a lifetime of debt. Back when we were in school, anyone could get a credit card. We'd fill out the applications in the student center just to get a free t-shirt. Bankruptcy was for later. We lived in the moment and didn't realize how screwed we were until we saw our first bill and learned to calculate a 20 percent interest rate.

Sure, the pandemic will leave us in a global recession unlike anything we've seen in modern times, but we've dug out of debt before, and we can do it again (did I mention we'll eat ramen and cereal for every meal?). My generation is uniquely qualified to make the best of this life, and it's a good thing because this has hit during our prime caretaking years. We have aging relatives and children who need us to be strong. It's a lot of responsibility, but we can handle it.

We're Gen X. We're here for you.

Or, you know, whatever...

6

HAPPY BIRTHDAYS AT HOME
MARY BETH

As a family, we're not big on birthdays. In fact, the kids don't have big birthday celebrations each year. There are simply too many of them. Instead, we celebrate quinquennial birthdays. It's not that we ignore their birthdays on off-years, but normally we only do quiet at-home celebrations. It's typical for us to buy a supermarket cake and make a favorite meal. But even with this little bit of effort, the April birthdays (Kate and Sadie) are usually the most haphazard of our efforts.

You see, Adam and I both teach at Youngstown State, and April in academia is jam-packed. In our household, having a birthday at the end of the Spring semester is pretty much the worst-case scenario. On top of work obligations, we get bogged down with the kids' school events, recitals, and other Spring shenanigans.

Overall, we do a poor job of celebrating.

Even when we do a bad job, Sadie and Kate don't mind so much. They know that once every five years, we'll pull out all the stops and deliver something spectacular. 2020 was supposed to be that spectacular year for Sadie. That's right, April 29 was Sadie's 10th birthday, and it should have been epic. Should have been, because the coronavirus stole her birthday.

If Sadie were Samantha in *Sixteen Candles*, she'd get to say, "The 'rona stole my friggin birthday." But, unlike Molly Ringwald's character, she's not alone in this disappointment because COVID-19 is disrupting a lot of people's birthdays.

For most of February, we were trying to decide between Dave & Buster's in Pittsburgh or a hotel sleepover pool party. But, before we even got an opportunity to call for pricing, the lockdown happened. Like a lot of kids (and adults), Sadie's birthday plans were destroyed.

Adam and I didn't come up with the concept of quinquennial birthday celebrations ourselves. We learned about them before we even started having kids. Three years prior to Ella's birth, while we were still graduate students, our media ethics professor at Kent State, Stan Wearden, introduced us to the concept.

Between teaching us about Just War Theory and Codes of Ethics, Wearden told our class about his family's philosophy regarding kids' parties. He and his wife saw how much time, money, and energy other families were spending on large celebrations (often for kids who wouldn't even remember) and decided to opt-out.

We didn't adopt this strategy right away, but around the time I got pregnant with Sadie we'd had enough. We have a drink in Stan's honor after each big birthday.

For us, big parties are just too much. Adam and I both work full-time and hosting an extravagant birthday every year for four children would have required the equivalent of a standing committee. As many parents know, it's a lot of work to pull off a kid's party.

Once you start inviting people, the guest list can get out of control. If you're a do-it-yourselfer, you end up spending late nights staring at Pinterest while baking and crafting. Some people love this, and for them, it's great, but I nearly lost my mind trying to make gift bags for a Little Mermaid-themed party at the Hubbard pool in 2010.

For us, the alternative to do-it-yourself parties was the quinquennial celebration. This allowed us the freedom to invest in pre-packaged birthdays. After I nearly ended it all under the sea, this became our go-to plan and a mouse by the name of Chuck E. Cheese was our main guy. Adam always opted for the high-end birthday package, complete with hats, noisemakers, balloons, and a seemingly endless supply of game tokens. He preferred footing the tab to the frenzy of harried party preparation done by two working, and not very crafty, parents.

In fact, he loved Chuck's so much he would slyly manipulate the kids into picking it. We're on a tight budget (student loans, mortgage, food for four growing kids), and a premium birthday package is not cheap, but when it was a once-in-five-years event, we could handle it. Mr. Cheese has made a lot of money off Earnheardt birthdays. The kids have the medals to prove it.

We always believed setting the birthday expectations in this way was a smart parenting choice. That belief held up until the coronavirus came to town. In our defense, when we decided to make the kids wait 5 years between birthday parties, there was no way to predict that our little Sadie Jay Bird would turn 10 during a global pandemic.

On the day the first stay-at-home orders were issued, we realized the implications right away. Stages of grief kicked in. Denial (no way Dave & Buster's will close), anger (this is bullshit), bargaining (April 29 is weeks away, we'll be able to do something fun), depression (everyone eats ice cream), and acceptance (we're gonna eat cake at the dining room table and open presents from Amazon).

As a family, we were at a loss about what to do for Sadie's big day. We asked for her input, and, in normal Sadie fashion, she was OK with whatever we decided. She's a good kid, follows rules, and trusts us to take care of her. She's not terribly outgoing, but she does have a nice batch of school friends. And, this was the year when she was supposed to be allowed to invite them to her birthday. And, that birthday was going to be fancy. She was supposed to get presents from someone other than her family. She was supposed to hear the voices of at least a dozen 10-year-olds singing "Happy Birthday." And, she was supposed to be the center of everyone's attention. No matter how sweet she was about canceling her plans, it still sucks to let your kid down.

The one bright spot was we were in a position to make it a multi-day celebration. Two days before Sadie's big day, Kate turned 13. Obviously, this one did not meet the requirement for a quinquennial fête, but it was still important because Kate has left her pre-teens and crossed into the teen years. So, we started on Monday with Chinese takeout, pizza, cupcakes, and presents for Kate. In a more hectic year, we would have crammed the girls' birthdays into one family party. This year we enjoyed celebrating them close together, yet separately.

For Sadie, we ordered takeout from her favorite, the Olive Garden (including 2 dozen breadsticks; if you do the math, that's four for each of us, but Sadie typically eats her weight in that salty bread). She and her brother had been saving for months to buy a Vector robot. Thankfully we had a few weeks to plan, so Adam was able to order it, and it arrived well before the big day. I made a terrible Jell-o cake at the birthday girl's request (she didn't request that it was terrible, just Jell-o).

We all sat around the dining room table enjoying each other's company. We ended the night with *The Masked Singer*, or as the kids call it, Furries Got Talent. I have no idea where they got the nickname. They may be creative, or it could be stolen from the world of online memes, or a shady school friend.

Like many other families during COVID, we weren't able to rely on our typical birthday routines. Still, we made the best of it. We'll give Sadie another shot at an epic party, and hopefully, we'll be celebrating a vaccine for the virus months before she makes it to eleven.

The pandemic has paused Sadie's big day, but it hasn't stopped her from celebrating. She had fun with her better-than-normal family party, and she enjoys being able to remind us that we still owe her one. Her anticipation for April 2021 helps us think past our current circumstances and the fun we have ahead. That's all we can expect from anyone right now, especially a newly minted 10-year-old.

7

(HOME)SCHOOL IS OUT FOR SUMMER

MARY BETH

We learned about a month ago that Ohio schools would not reopen for face-to-face learning for the rest of the academic year. As soon as the news was announced, our teenagers and their friends began sharing text messages of joy. In an act of sibling solidarity, the older kids told the little ones, and the four Earnheardt children celebrated their good fortune as if they were Cleveland Browns fans finally winning a Superbowl. I swear they nearly blew the roof off the house.

"It's summer vacation," Oscar said. "A whole month early."

I wish I could say Adam and I felt as happy about the news, but we did not. The next month would be anything but a vacation for us. By the time the governor made the announcement, the novelty of helping our kids with lessons had worn off and we were in the weeds. We had been desperately hoping that the schools would re-open and we'd get a break.

After the initial disappointment, Adam and I came up with a plan. The older kids were easy. From the start, the teenagers were much more engaged with their learning. Ella and Kate used the school-provided Chromebooks to access their classrooms and teachers. Ella is naturally responsible and had been writing all of her assignments on her own personal whiteboard since before school closed. Every night at dinner, she gave detailed descriptions of the work she'd completed, reports on outstanding assignments, and a timeline for ongoing projects.

Ella will be an excellent CEO someday.

Our middle daughter Kate didn't appear to be doing any work at all. She spent a lot of time in her room, lying on her bed, looking at memes. In a brilliant move of delegation, we assigned her to Ella for tending, and Ella added information about Kate's progress to the daily reports.

According to Ella, Kate was doing work and passing all her classes. Ella said, "I procrastinate. Kate does not." I guess we'll find out when the final grades are posted next week. If either of them ends up in summer school, we'll know we dropped the ball, but we feel pretty confident they are doing great.

The truth is, our teenagers have always been motivated to work on their assignments. They figured out early that the quicker their work was done, the sooner they'd be back to watching YouTube and texting friends.

Oscar was our real challenge. He was hard to manage, but at least his workload was relatively easy. We made a schedule for him, and, with constant supervision, he completed a few pages of his packet each day. Once we found out how to motivate him, our supervisory duties were less arduous. The trick was reminding him that the less he screwed around, the more time he'd have for his true passion — playing Minecraft.

We set Sadie up in a similar way. She had designated learning times and we made sure one of us was available for questions and moral support. The first few days went so well, we figured she knew what she was doing and let her do it. Turns out, this was a mistake.

On the Friday before the first set of packets were due, Adam searched the house looking for Sadie's "learning nests." He pulled papers from behind the sofa, beside the computer, on the dining room mantel, and various spots in her bedroom.

Once they were assembled, Adam discovered the truth. Most of Sadie's work was not done. Despite our early, good intentions, we had gotten distracted with our full-time jobs and left a fourth-grader with encouraging words and not much else. We hoped for the best but got burned by this strategy when we saw page after page of blank worksheets. Turns out she hadn't been doing much for at least 3 weeks, which was confusing because it looked like she was working every day.

As a result of her daydreaming, she spent an entire weekend catching up on four packets. Adam monitored her progress. It took about eight hours and was grueling work. He got to witness first-hand just how easy it was for his youngest daughter to zone out, and he needed to administer constant reminders to keep her on task. I'm happy to report that Sadie's most recent set of packets were all done on time and turned in without incident. Although, this has more to do with her teachers holding daily Zoom meetings than Adam and I monitoring her progress.

In addition to our lack of engagement, we also found that the weather interfered with homeschool plans. Much of April and May was unseasonably warm and sunny. Aside from a day or two of snow in May (welcome to northeast Ohio), the nice days and sunshine coupled with the lack of "real school" messed with our children's heads, tripping an internal switch that signaled summer vacation.

This set off a change in attitude and appearance. The children have stopped wearing proper clothing. In related news, I have completed all the laundry in the house for the first time since 2005, which is possible if the children wear the same pajamas for three days straight. We have to remind them to shower, and we don't have a lot of credibility on the subject since our social isolation hygiene isn't as good as it should be.

We've been reading online that it can be good to try to stick to your normal routine as a way to create structure for the day. We tried this for a few weeks, but it's just not us. We're not the type of family that's going to wake up, shower, and get dressed just to sit at home. When we're home, we like to be comfortable. I mean, why sit at the dining room table during normal school hours, if you can lay in your bed and text your friends? Even Adam and I are taking Zoom meetings from the comfort of our bedroom.

Now that we're nearing the end of the school year, we've established some loose routines that fit us as a family, and I hope we can keep it up during real summer vacation. At least once a week, Adam, the kids, and I watch some of Gov. Mike DeWine's press conferences. I like the idea of having my family gather around the television with a bunch of other Ohioans and acknowledging that we're #InThisTogetherOhio.

The kids have been interested because they have another connection to the press conferences. Ohio Department of Health Director, Dr. Amy Acton is a graduate of Liberty High School and because this is their school, my kids think she is very cool. The information Dr. Acton shares in the press conferences is helpful and she makes us all feel a little bit better. Plus, she's the one who signed the order that got the kids out of school and that's the kind of power move they respect.

In pre-pandemic days, we'd be going to picnics and signing field trip permission slips. Instead, we're building dams in the creek and eating breakfast for dinner several nights a week. We've learned that we're an informal kind of family, but that our informality doesn't get in the way of learning and being productive. We're learning how to step up and be responsible for ourselves. Instead of fitting in, being at home for work and play has shown us how we naturally like to exist.

I don't know what a pandemic summer vacation will look like. But it's likely to be lazier than in past years. We're probably going to figure out how to have fun without going anywhere. We may finally get around to cleaning out some rooms and donating items we've outgrown.

And, someday, we'll get word that the schools are reopened. When that day comes, we'll have to adjust again, or maybe, everyone else will agree to just wear their pajamas all day, too.

8

DYADS AND SINGLETONS
MARY BETH

We left the kids alone for about seven hours so we could work on a project in Pennsylvania.

We left at 6 a.m. Blankets were folded. The dishes were done. Coats were hung up. All major surfaces were clear of debris.

When we returned, it looked like a bomb exploded. There was foam packaging material torn to tiny bits in every room. Blankets, pillows, coats, and towels were piled on the floor. The cupboard was bare of clean dishes and the dirty ones filled the countertops and coffee table.

I'm not sure you could pay a group of children to make a larger mess in such short order.

On days like this, I really wish I lived alone. I dream about an alternate universe where I clean my house and it stays clean. I remember hearing from my single friends when the stay-at-home order was first put in place. They had cleaned out closets and donated items they didn't use. Their residences were never cleaner. Instagram documented their hard work.

But in the homes of families with small children, the opposite is happening. Our closets have never been messier. Attempts to get rid of old items are met with cries of terror from tiny hoarders.

Sure, even in pre-pandemic days, our place was teeming with children. But in 2020, the kids are always here, and our poor house has never been more lived in. At least in pre-pandemic days, there were sleepovers and playdates and 5-day-a-week school schedules. In 2020, it's all-kids, all-day, all-night, in every nook and cranny of our seemingly shrinking square footage.

And if there's no kid in said nook or cranny, there's a dog (or two with an occasional cat who comes out of hiding at snack time).

Because of this, I often get frustrated. This is not my normal frustration, it's a much deeper feeling of hopelessness and desperation. I long for the days when we would put them on the bus and have a few minutes to clean up messes. But now, with the positive COVID case counts going in the wrong direction, as the fall season wanes and winter sets in, I feel the weight of even more long days in our unharmonious living situation.

I know I could make the kids more responsible. I do try, but when you are operating out of chaos, with job and family obligations wearing you down, it's hard to fight all the time.

The only coping mechanism I have that seems to help is imagining how lonely COVID would be if they weren't here.

Everyone suffers a bit from the belief that the grass is always greener. We believe that our problems would magically disappear if we went someplace else. We look at our partners and think that other mates wouldn't take us for granted. We assume people in different homes and living situations are getting through this period of isolation without feeling hopeless.

Under our current circumstances, it's easier than ever to do this. Those of us who haven't been alone for more than a few minutes since early March are looking for solitude, while many of us who have been in solitude are desperately seeking some company. The thing about COVID is that it reduces our normal circumstances and increases the intensity.

One of our natural family patterns that has intensified is our tendency to split into pairs. I'm not sure how we began this, although Adam theorized it's a legacy of assigning riding partners at amusement parks. In most all our adventures, we end up with our normal partners.

We have four mostly happy twosomes that make up these smaller units (Mom/Dad, big kids, littles, dogs). Living as dyads is now a normal part of our lives.

A dyad is the smallest form of a social group. According to Wikipedia, "The strength of the relationship is evaluated on the basis of time the individuals spend together, as well as on the emotional intensity of their relationship." This part of the definition explains why our pairing off is even more noticeable. We are spending a lot of time together and because of this, we're taking more responsibility than ever for each other's emotions.

Our youngest children, Sadie and Ozzie, are usually very good about playing together. They occasionally dust-up, but it's not a big deal. Since the lockdown has increased their time together, their feuds are more brutal than they once were. A minor slight can be combustible enough to cause a massive set of dueling meltdowns. It's hard for me or Adam to adjudicate these disputes while we're trying to host a WebEx meeting.

This brings me to the next part of the Wikipedia definition: "A dyad can be unstable because both persons must cooperate to make it work. If one of the two fails to complete their duties, the group would fall apart." Some days we just don't want to do our part. This applies to the kids as well as the grown-ups. It's in these times that we long for distance from each other. A few hours to live like a singleton (a term I learned from Helen Fielding's "Bridget Jones's Diary" and have since loved).

From the messy, combative inside of my house, I can't help but think that those who live in their own space, who can create a harmonious environment, have greener grass. I find myself dreaming about little things like peanut butter without finger marks and visiting with my friends on Zoom without needing to mediate a battle over who should have control of the remote.

There's only one way to make it to the other side of the pandemic, and that is to go through it. Surviving it. There's no life hack or special trick anyone can use to avoid the journey we're all on together. And even though we can't control our current circumstances, it does help to look at your grass from the other side of the fence.

When I long for a few hours of alone time, I try to remember how lucky I am to get goodnight snuggles (even from a kid who hasn't bathed in days). And I hope that reading about my chaos reminds those of you who may be feeling lonely to try and treasure the peace.

9
FAMILY MOURNING IN A PANDEMIC

MARY BETH

2020 broke my heart.

We hadn't even made it to April and it was already feeling like the year of missed opportunities, canceled events, and isolation. Sure, most of this stuff we could celebrate virtually, or put off to another day. But death is hard to deal with over text messages.

Saying goodbye to someone you love is hard even in the best of times. Saying goodbye today, in the midst of a pandemic, is a mess, especially for those who don't have a long history of dealing with this type of grief.

I've been trying to decide if this topic is appropriate for a column about parenting during the pandemic, but it's the only thing occupying my mind these days. It involves some recent losses we're facing as a family and how Adam, the kids, and I are trying to cope with them.

I'm sure my kids are doing cute and funny things, mostly to make me stop crying, but it's hard for me to be observant about this stuff right now.

In March and April, three of my aunts died. When we hear the title "Aunt," I think it can be easy to dismiss it. It doesn't carry the weight of the nuclear family, like brother or mother. But, if you are in a close family, you know just how important these women are. And losing even one of them would have been a tragedy. Losing three so closely together is staggering.

"Aunts have long served as sources of material aid to families in need of support," wrote Laura Ellingson and Patricia Sotirin in their book *Aunting: Cultural Practices that Sustain Family and Cultural Life.*

"The babysitting aunt, the 'rich' benefactress aunt, the aunt who sponsors the immigration of the rest of the family ... as an embodiment of a family and cultural heritage, or as people who help maintain extended family ties," Ellingson and Sotirin added. "Aunting is shaped by circumstances as much as we enact it in ways that respond to those circumstances."

I don't have to look far to see that I'm not alone in the weight of loss. A pandemic brings waves of it and in most cases, it's the older who are vulnerable.

Many of us lost people, and it hurts. Unlike the stories I see featured on the news, no diagnoses are linking the deaths in my family to the coronavirus, but when all this was happening in 2020, the causes and circumstances of their deaths didn't really matter to me. I was simply trying to grasp the fact that while I was sheltering in place, the people who I love were slipping away.

Instead of being able to leave my normal life and gather with family to say goodbye, we continued to work from home, on laptops, wearing masks, staying distant, and isolating.

Mourning in a pandemic sucks.

So, because I didn't get a chance to honor them properly in the traditions that bring me comfort, I'm going to take a few sentences to tell you about my aunts.

Aunt Mary talked slowly and abundantly. She liked to tell a story and took the long road to the point, but if you followed along with her, there were rewards. She was wise and kind and I loved it when she laughed. She also made the best desserts I'll ever eat. Period.

Aunt Karen was the tiniest grownup in my family, but she also had the biggest personality. She was funny and nurtured everyone she met. Aunt Karen was magnetic, and this quality caused her to create community wherever she went. She was born to be center stage. In fact, she once applied to be a contestant for the reality show *Survivor* and came very close to battling for the $1 million prize. I'm still convinced she would've won.

Aunt Donny was a second mother to me, and an additional grandmother to my children. She could be cranky and a bit too serious, but she loved us deeply (almost as much as she loved *Family Feud*). When it felt like the world was falling apart, she was the one who would tell us that we were all overreacting and that we just needed to get on with life. We all could use more Aunt Donny right now, but we lost her in April.

For many families, children are introduced to death through ritual. They get dressed up to attend viewings and funerals and learn how to pay their respects. It's a time for kids to meet the extended family who made the trip to say goodbye. They get to put a face to people that before they had only heard stories about. Even though it's painful, the rituals we associate with death are a coping mechanism and give us a foundation on which we can build healing.

My kids missed these important rituals during social distancing.

When Aunt Mary died, we were not yet under lockdown, so we made the trip home to attend viewing hours. Ella was the only one who accompanied Adam and I to the funeral home. I was going to take the whole Earnheardt gang to the memorial service, but, even though it was just a short time after the viewing, we missed it because of the state-issued shelter-in-place orders.

We missed the eulogies. We missed seeing the people who loved her, giving hugs, holding their hands, and sharing important stories. We missed sharing the tears and laughter that come with remembering.

By the time Aunt Karen died, we were further into isolation. It feels especially sad that she didn't get to have a large funeral because she was a superstar and loved a party (her children have mentioned a memorial when it becomes feasible). I told my kids about Aunt Karen at the dinner table, and then we ate chicken nuggets. It wasn't a proper way for them to understand the impact her life had on the family. While we ride out the uncertainty, Aunt Karen's children set up a Facebook memorial site so we can use social media to connect. I love seeing photos of her and reading the other posts, but I usually do this alone, away from the children.

Aunt Donny died on a Tuesday morning. Nephews, nieces and cousins wanted to come home to say goodbye, but we had to keep it small. The funeral director said what anyone would expect. "Only very small gatherings with masks, hand sanitizer, and proper social distance."

Those last two words would certainly be the challenge: social distance. For most people who are in emotional pain, there is a longing for closeness. We are drawn to others like magnets and need to be close to each other for emotional support. These days, our magnets are more like those we're trying to connect with similar poles--we're purposely pushing each other away to protect ourselves and prevent the spread of this horrible virus.

I'm heartbroken that my children won't have the experiences of saying goodbye that I took for granted, the ceremonies that turn the pain of missing someone into a celebration of a life well-lived. I'm sad for myself that I won't get to see my large collection of cousins and look through scrapbooks and pictures, and tell stories.

But one of the things that brings me comfort is that under all the pain this pandemic is causing, there seems to be genuine kindness and understanding because we're all in this together. I saw it in social media posts, I read it in my text messages, and I heard it during phone conversations. Many people were coping with this crazy year by being compassionate.

Sure, our losses are different. Some of us lost our wedding receptions, or a job, or a year of sports, or a graduation ceremony. It's not the same as death, but it still hurts. The only way through this was to be there for each other. Pain doesn't have to be ranked and sorted; it needs to be acknowledged.

And in dealing with the pain, many of us found common ground. We were there for each other because we collectively mourned for things that could have been but were not.

Yep, 2020 broke my heart, but at least I wasn't alone.

10

WHEN THE KIDS PLANNED PANDEMIC DATE NIGHTS

MARY BETH

Recently, I challenged the kids to plan two pandemic date nights for Adam and I.

The rules were simple. They'd form two teams. Each team would be responsible for one date. The date night budget was set at $50, and we would order/buy any supplies they required, no questions asked. The date had to last a minimum of two hours and happen on or before April 15.

There are three reasons why I did this. First, Adam and I have always tried to prioritize romance. We've done this by setting boundaries and making it a family priority to keep Mom and Dad in love (I know, kinda gross; that last part often elicits a well-deserved "ewww" from our children). We go on regular dates. We cuddle and kiss in front of the kids. We do all the yucky stuff we think they need to see so that they grow up with an appreciation of what a healthy and loving partnership looks like.

Second, the pandemic has created a situation where our family feels a bit out of control. Like many people, we've changed our behaviors to accommodate restrictions on movement while still trying to maintain some normalcy in our homes. We've started wearing masks when we go out. Our bedrooms are now offices and schools. When we visit Adam's mom, it's to wave from our minivan, parked a safe distance from her front door.

Even under these conditions, as adults, we're able to find parts of life we can still control. But for the most part, children don't have this luxury. They don't get to decide when it's time to go to the store. They've been forced to go to class over Zoom on days and times set by their teachers. Their only playdates are with their siblings and occasionally Dad if it means teaching him how to play Animal Crossing and Minecraft on the Nintendo Switch.

The kids have to trust that all the layers of authority who are responsible for them know the best strategies for keeping them safe. So, by allowing our kids the freedom to plan a date night for us, we gave them a little bit of control.

Finally, there's not much going on around here and I thought "pandemic date night" would be a cute concept to write about.

I announced the date night about a week ago and was surprised when they immediately went to work.

Team Kate and Sadie jumped on the computer and started yelling out suspicious questions.

"Do you like seafood?"

"What's the name of that bread you got mad at Mom for not buying?"

"Do we have to worry about calories?"

"On a scale of 1-10, how much do you like *Star Wars*?"

These were good and thoughtful questions, which prompted Adam to say, "I think my heart is gonna burst, in a good way."

They began crafting the perfect evening, although truth be told, I wondered how Adam and I would complete their itinerary in two hours. Let's just say that bread, a walk, dinner, crafts, stand-up comedy, wine, karaoke, and Netflix seemed like an ambitious agenda for a couple in their late-40s.

Seeing them have fun working together and making plans made me excited. They wanted the night to be special.

Team Ella and Ozzie had something romantic and a little more decadent in store for us. Their plan required that a fondue pot be purchased on Amazon. Considering Amazon's shipping delays during the pandemic, we were uncertain if they could pull this off before the deadline. But, instead of hitting them in the face with a lesson in the realities of Amazon Prime's ground shipping, we said nothing, and thankfully we were fondue-ready in just a few days.

After some arguing between teams on what night each date would take place, the evenings were set. Team Ella and Ozzie went on Saturday. Team Katie and Sadie went on Monday.

Saturday night delivered on the romantic promise of a date. The basement was cleared of all toys, and a meal of spaghetti, bread, grapes, and chocolate fondue let off a rich aroma. It was all about atmosphere and ambiance. We sat in a nest of blankets (and literally every pillow we own) while we ate. Yankee candles burned all around us, and when dinner was over, Ella and Oz set up a movie for us to watch.

They quizzed us both and correctly surmised that we like horror. After researching the plots on IMDB, they downloaded 1922 from Netflix, careful to make sure our spotty Wi-Fi didn't interfere with our enjoyment. I was relaxing, and Adam and I had a good time.

Monday night was equally as successful, but it was a more raucous affair. Like the other date, it started with some serious preparation. Sadie cleared off the table, picked flowers, and sprayed everything down with Febreze. The $50 budget was spent on takeout from our favorite Mexican restaurant, Senor Jalapeño in Liberty.

After dinner, Adam and I did crafts while Kate and Sadie took turns reading aloud from Marx's *Communist Manifesto* (don't judge; they thought it was funny). Then we went for a 5-minute jog-walk around the house while the kids set up for a standup comedy show which consisted of jokes taken from the internet (my fave: "A lady at the bank asked me to check her balance so I knocked her over"). After standup, we all joined in for karaoke which culminated with

Adam and I singing "I Had the Time of My Life," while the kids danced. I don't think I've laughed that hard in months.

Turns out the pandemic date nights were a great distraction for the whole family. The kids had a blast planning and executing them, and their hard work was rewarded with a sense of accomplishment.

In fact, they did such a great job that when we go back to normal life, Adam and I are seriously considering letting them plan all future birthdays and vacations.

11

UNINTENDED CONSEQUENCES
OF UNINVITED GUESTS

MARY BETH

L ast week, attorney Rod Ponton appeared in a Texas court looking like a kitten. The court was meeting online, and the judge and others were unable to help Mr. Ponton. He didn't consciously choose to appear as a kitten. He reported that a filter setting was changed on his computer without his knowledge, and he didn't know how to correct the problem.

Who would do such a thing to this poor man, you ask?

The answer won't surprise any of the parents reading this column. Ponton had lent his computer to his child. I found Ponton's story relatable.

The pandemic has brought parenting into the professional world in the most unprofessional ways. It has allowed those of you who don't have small children at home to see behind the curtain of those of us who do. As a working parent, it's a curtain I work very hard to keep closed. Tightly closed. Like blackout closed.

Some parents feel differently and regularly share their children with the world. I admire them, but it's just not for me. The people around me don't judge, and my (very patient, supportive) colleagues have always been kind about my children. They ask about them and make genuinely thoughtful comments about how big and beautiful and smart they are.

But no matter what they say, my inner critic always thinks, "How can anyone respect me if they see the unseriousness of my personal life?" Even writing this column can be hard because it's a glimpse inside our chaotic home life. The main difference is the level of control. In normal times (i.e., pre-, and, one day, post-pandemic), I decide what to share and how and when to share it.

The curtain is open for a few minutes but then yanked tightly back in place before I get too uncomfortable.

It's the times when I screw up while working from home that make me cringe. When I'm in a meeting, I don't want anyone to think of me as a mother. I don't want anyone to see just beyond the edges of the video, where one slight tilt to the left will show a massive pile of dirty clothes, and a tilt to the right will reveal one of our kids picking a nose (and maybe not his own) or flipping a middle finger just for the fun of it.

My children always seem to have different agendas and motives. Because I'm at home, they don't seem to understand that I need to be a professional. Who can blame them? I don't take my children to work with me, not even on our annual "take your kids to work" day. Before the pandemic, I did almost all of my work in the office. It was a firm boundary that has now been smashed to smithereens.

Mostly the kids are good at letting me alone, with one exception. Our son, Ozzie, looks for opportunities to interrupt work and upend the seriousness. He's a clown and he knows it. He's an entertainer. For him, people on the other side of a WebEx meeting aren't my co-workers. They're just another potential audience for his high jinks and crass humor.

Adam and I work in the same department at Youngstown State. Because of this, we often find ourselves attending online meetings together. It's a tough situation to work through when the kids are remote schooling from home. When we're both on, we're both engaged with work, and there's no adult to entertain (i.e., distract) the little ones.

In a recent college-wide meeting, Ozzie discovered how power-less we were. He found me in the kitchen giving a report and peeked over my shoulder to see Adam as one of the other participants. When he saw his dad, it was only a few seconds before he realized that Adam was online in another room.

Ozzie ran from me to Adam. Soon his face was pressed against Adam's in the tiny online window. When I was done talking, Ozzie was back with me (waving from stage left with a cheesy grin; and by "cheesy grin," I mean he literally had cheeseball powder crusted around the ring of his mouth). He proceeded to run between the two of us for at least 20 minutes until I bribed him with a cupcake.

Thank God for the mute button and Little Debbie's cupcakes. Because this screen bombing was a new occurrence, Adam and I had no predetermined deterrence strategy.

We were sitting ducks, and Ozzie knew it.

But, if we weren't on a work call, we would have been able to use our normal strategy of yelling at him. This is a little something my friend, Tiffany Anderson, calls "bringing the thunder." I'm not proud to admit it, but on occasion, I yell at the kids. Adam does too. We probably do it more often than we should, but at times it can feel like tone and volume are the only way to break through the complete disregard for what we're saying.

Yelling at your child isn't the same as raising your voice to another adult. With the exception of Adam, no one in my life ignores what I say quite the way the children do. It's like the fact that they incubated in my body has filled them with immunity to my words. Even when I yell, they mostly manage to ignore me.

But, in the professional environment, I can't yell. Even if muted, if I did yell, I would look like a crazy person and likely make my coworkers uncomfortable. Most HR departments prefer a less forceful form of mediation. But, in my experience, a reasoned approach just doesn't penetrate the noggin of an 8-year-old. So, instead of turning away from the camera and going full mom on Oz, I just try to smile through his shenanigans and hope I don't look like a complete idiot (or worse, a pushover).

I'm still thankful I remembered the cupcakes.

It's not just the antics of an 8-year-old that throw me off my game. Just like Mr. Ponton, I sometimes let the kids use my work laptop for school. I probably shouldn't do this, but when you have four children in online meetings, you need a fallback plan. You need multiple devices. We mostly manage (thankfully, Liberty Local Schools lends middle- and high-schoolers Chromebooks to use during the school year).

Once in a while, something breaks down and I don't even think about my work. I just respond to the emergency of getting the child-in-need-of-tech into a Google hangout, albeit on my work computer.

This is completely acceptable until a kid tinkers with settings on your work laptop (e.g., Mr. Ponton) or randomly dismisses or deletes an "alert" for a meeting, which was my dilemma last week. I received a call from work asking why I wasn't "on" an online meeting. I felt like the kid who gets called out by the teacher in front of the whole class. My face flushed and I had to summon deep reserves of courage to enter the call late.

My colleagues were very kind, but I still felt like I let everyone down. And yes, I blamed it on the kid. Why not? These days, the "my kid did it" excuse is as commonplace as "I can't get my camera to work."

There's something deeply humanizing for all of us when we log into our professional lives from our personal spaces. We see glimpses of people we think we know. People who are trying to present themselves as best they can. And, sometimes the presentation falls apart or is sabotaged by a little kid holding chocolate cupcakes (yes, he found a way to leverage a second treat during our online meeting).

I don't know what it will be like when we resume less-online lives, but I am looking forward to restoring some boundaries.

In the meantime, I appreciate the kindness and patience of my colleagues and friends. I appreciate the ways in which their lives have changed and understand that the curtain can't stay as tightly closed as some of us would prefer.

I am hopeful that this will make me less concerned about showing myself as a mother, and build my comfort level in both worlds. After all, we're all in this together, and the occasional kid or critter who pops up in a Zoom call is sometimes a welcome distraction during the virtual workday.

12

WHEN PUPPIES NAMED FOR VILLIANS TURN ANTISOCIAL

MARY BETH

Raising a puppy is hard work. Raising two puppies at the same time is harder work. Raising two puppies at the same time during a pandemic is insanity.

We got the puppies for the children. Years of pleas and promises led us to the decision to expand our family. Adam and I deliberated and negotiated until we reached an agreement. We spit on our hands and shook (before the pandemic, of course; no spit shakes these days) and put deposits down on two puppies in July 2019.

The terms were as follows:

1. There would be two, preferably littermates (my negotiating point). I learned from having four children that everyone is a little less annoying if they have someone to play with.

2. They would be large dogs (Adam's point). He's a big guy (6-feet-8-inches) and wanted a dog to scale. Let's see him handle two in a few years.

3. With parental guidance, the kids would walk, feed, cuddle, bathe, train, and meet all the canine needs of the two new Earn-heardts (family covenant, not to be broken without serious repercussions, or, as it turns out, zero repercussions).

With the terms clearly defined, it was time to determine names. This is typically a stressful occurrence in large families. Everyone wants naming privileges, and the process can get nasty. We still have residual bad feelings over naming our cat nearly four years ago. Our black and white purr machine is named Jaws, but Team Oreo (Sadie) still has resentments. I remind her that "Oreo" was a terrible name because every time we said it, her then-3-year-old brother would ask for a cookie.

Jaws' name was determined by letting each family member decide on four names. After we had our field, we used bracketed voting to get the final two, Jaws and Oreo. Then we put these on social media and let our friends and family weigh in. Voting was fair and square and, much to my relief, we were able to maintain the Earnheardt tradition of naming our pets after pop-culture villains and monsters.

That's right, sometime about 20 years ago, Adam and I decided there was nothing more adorable than a baby animal with the name of a bad guy. We started with Keyser Soze (i.e., the villain from *The Usual Suspects*) Earnheardt, a skittish, beautiful yellow dog Adam gave me as a wedding present. Then it was Godzilla Earnheardt, a strange little tortie kitten. After that, it was Sméagol (a.k.a. Gollum) Earnheardt, who had a permanent smile and curly tail. We thought we were done, but to curry favor with a professor in graduate school, we took in the feral feline, Rodan Earnheardt, fittingly named for one of Godzilla's nemeses.

And, of course, Jaws. The only exceptions to the naming rule were Sandy and Abby who came to us as older and already named dogs.

The names never fit the personalities of our animals. Although we named them after baddies and beasts, they were anything but mean — all-loving, four-legged family members who want nothing more than a full belly and an occasional ear scratch.

We learned from our mistakes last time and decided this time we would use a ranked-choice voting process (female choices finalized

by me and male by Adam) that resulted in Iago the Doggo (Iggy) and
Lady Macbeth (Mickey) Earnheardt — famous Shakespearean
villains.

In mid-November, we drove 3.5 hours to the center of Pennsylvania to pick up our new family members, in an area so rural that our
GPS was certain we made a wrong turn and assumed we were in
New Jersey. At the time, with our work schedules and the kids in
school, we were worried about being gone from home too many
hours during the day to adequately train them.

It turns out, because of the pandemic, we now have a different
problem: our Shakespearean villains are becoming horribly
antisocial.

They didn't start this way. According to experts, the sweet spot
for socializing puppies is between 9 and 12 weeks, and we honored
their teachings by ensuring Iggy and Mickey were out and about,
meeting other people, and getting used to the world around them.
Then right about the time the pups turned 6 months, COVID-19
disrupted puppy life.

Walks in the park and visits with extended family stopped.
Doggy play dates were canceled. The dogs were trapped with us, and
we were trapped with the dogs and that's pretty much where we are
today. With all the social distancing and closings, we don't have
many opportunities to take them places where they can interact with
other animals and people.

The progress we were making in socializing them is now undone,
as they've been thrust into a world where nearly all interaction is
limited to their mixed human-canine-feline pack.

Mickey is doing all right. She's always been a little more coura-
geous and was easier to train, but Iggy is a terror. Even the distant
sight of our friendly neighbors sends him into a barking fit (apolo-
gies to Jan and Evelyn, Mary, John, and "the boys"). Delivery drivers
are greeted with menacing growls. My mother-in-law's boyfriend is
treated like persona non grata. In fairness to Iggy, you just can't get a

good, proper sniff at folks when they have to stay 6 feet away, and in a dog's world, odor is everything.

It might bring the humans comfort to know that Iggy is antisocial around other animals, too. Foreign dogs, cats, squirrels, and chipmunks are essentially terrorists who must be stopped at all costs (from a distance, preferably while hiding behind one of the human children). The only animals that still confound Iggy and Mickey are city deer. The dogs aren't sure if they should bark, bow, chase, or sniff.

I find Iggy's antisocial behavior upsetting because when he's alone with us, he's the most adorable, loving puppy a family could want, and I worry that I'm missing my chance to get him ready to greet the world with wonder and curiosity. It was just a few months ago when the sight of someone new piqued his interest but now it scares him. Even on rare occasions when we venture to the park and find other dogs, social distancing rules prohibit friendly butt-sniffing. Turns out that whether I'm dog-momming or human-momming, I'm worried about the long-term effects this messed-up world will have on my little ones.

Like other adjustments I've made in my daily routines, I know the problems we're facing with our socially-distanced puppies won't last forever. And, according to news reports, dog adoptions are on the rise because many people are at home right now. So, I'm sure that when we hit the dog park, there will be other dogs who are cautiously optimistic about making new friends.

In the meantime, when I set aside the shedding and pooping and peeing and yapping and stealing food and farting and eating shoes and licking faces and getting up at 5 a.m. (did I mention pooping?), now is a nice time for new puppies. We have time for them and the only thing a puppy really wants from a human is time.

I just hope when we return to normal and get them socialized with the rest of the world, we'll have formed new, better human habits, and that these habits will include lots of long, lazy afternoons with our dogs.

13

ISO A PANDEMIC HOUSEKEEPER

MARY BETH

S everal years ago, when we started having kids and the burden of a never-ending list of chores was threatening the stability of our marriage, Adam suggested that we hire a housekeeper.

He'd say stuff like, "Hey, I see there's a Molly Maid right up the street," or "You seem so tired from taking care of the kids. We could get help with some of the house stuff. Ya know, just the things we can't get to."

Every time he tried, I shot down that idea. It's not that I don't love the idea of a clean house, or that I think there's something wrong with hiring domestic help. Adam and I and many members of our families have done housekeeping work for cash in the past. It's just that I can't imagine having a stranger in my house, moving from room to room, seeing our life for the complete chaos that it is.

The way we live is just too embarrassing.

Aside from the fact that I'd be embarrassed, I also have financial concerns. I knew we couldn't afford it on our salaries back then. Now, with four kids, I'm convinced we can't afford it (even though, admittedly, neither one of us has really checked the going rate for a housekeeper).

I am notoriously tight with the purse strings. You can thank my childhood best friend, my grandma, for these views. She lived through the depression and was married to a man who had a job through Roosevelt's WPA. She would butter pieces of thick home-made bread, heat a little milk on the stove, and drench the bread with it. Then she'd hit it with a little salt and pepper and serve it to me. She called it milk soup and it was delicious. This was not the only meatless dish my grandma made me from her collection of depression-era recipes.

I'm starting to think all the depression-influenced training of my youth may come in handy with the state of the economy. A year ago, I might have considered a housekeeper, but under these circum-stances, there is no way I'm willing to shell out money to have someone else clean my house.

Still, there are days I wish I had someone to help.

Since we all started sheltering in place, our shelter has turned into a hell hole.

It's difficult to move through this house without finding at least one room that isn't or hasn't recently been occupied. If a room is occupied, it either A) smells like someone who hasn't bathed recently, B) has dirty clothes strewn from couches and computer monitors, C) has empty, half-crushed pop cans with missing tabs (see last week's column), dirty dishes or paper plates (or some scien-tific experiments stuck to end tables and other furniture), or D) all or some combination of all of the above.

If a room isn't occupied, see A through D above, but add in E) lights are on and/or F) electronics are still on.

We're always in a state of competition with the kids. I banish them from the room I'm cleaning with the knowledge that wherever they take up residence will be destroyed next. It's a game of whack-a-mole. Every time I knock one mole down, multiple heads that pop up in the other holes. The only way to get ahead is to clean when the kids are otherwise occupied outside the house. I'd get a chance to mop the floors while Ozzie was at the YMCA playing basketball. I would change the bedding on days when Ella and Katie were at afterschool activities. It wasn't perfect, but it worked.

Adam was desperate before the pandemic, but now he's downright apoplectic. Recently, he collapsed on our bed and told me to watch as he keyed the letters, M-O-L-L-Y... and before he was even done typing, it appeared as the number one option, as if the Google Gods knew my deepest, darkest desires.

Their opening page is quite alluring. The one line that got me was, "Your home should feel like an escape from the pressures of everyday life." Amen, sister.

I would like an escape. Heck, I'd settle for walking through the living room without a Lego injury to the foot. But even if I let Adam click the button and hire some help, I don't think I'd be any more relaxed about it.

You see, when he was a young adult, Adam lived with his Aunt Dottie, and she had a housekeeper. He knows that a little help can go a long way, but he also knows that his aunt made him help her clean before the cleaning lady arrived. This makes complete sense to me, but it also strengthens the argument against hiring help. I think it would be more stressful to know I had to clean because a housekeeper was coming over to clean. Also, I think I'd probably insist on helping. I'd end up just being a nuisance to a perfectly capable housekeeper.

For now, we've resigned ourselves to living in filth. We smile kindly when a relative who doesn't have kids at home brags about how many bags they've donated to Goodwill, or posts pictures of rooms and closets they've cleaned out during the pandemic.

For now, I'll keep making my arguments for why we can't afford to hire someone and how much anxiety it would cause me, but living like this has made me more open to the idea.

For now, I think I'll try teaching the kids to clean (for the 1,000th time). If that doesn't work, I may just let Adam win this one.

14

IN THE NOSE OF THE BEHOLDER

MARY BETH

"When was the last time you showered?" Adam asked Ozzie last week while he searched our living room for the origins of an awful smell. The rest of us just sat there nonplussed. Adam does this all the time.

"Tuesday? I think," Ozzie replied. "What day is it?"

"Today is Sunday," Adam answered.

Ozzie looked down at his body, still in the same PJs from three days ago, tucked his nose under the top of his shirt, and took a deep sniff. "I smell OK," he said with a wry smile.

The truth is, Ozzie didn't smell OK. He hadn't showered in several days because days blend together during the pandemic. It's likely that Adam already knew the source of the stench, but he wanted to hear Ozzie cop to it.

You see, Adam has notoriously impressive olfaction. I swear he's like a bloodhound. Like a canine with its snout in the air, he'll walk around the house taking rapid-fire sniffs, occasionally holding up clothing, towels, stuffed animals, and other paraphernalia to his nose in hopes of isolating problem areas.

If there were a body in the woods, Adam would find it quicker than a cadaver dog. Sometimes when I see him on a quest to sniff out an odor the rest of us don't smell, I wonder if other people smell us the way Adam does. He tells me that he recalls memories by their smells. His childhood home. An old church. Locker rooms. His Mother's break-up-and-bread-eggs. Istanbul. The delivery rooms where our children were born. Cook Forest near Clarion, Pa. His Aunt Patty's perfume. Each place and person and time came with unique smells that correlate with a memory, some happy, some sad, and some which would otherwise be forgettable if not for his sense of smell.

Lately, I've been thinking about the smell of our house. This is probably because I've been spending 23.50 hours a day for 4-plus months banging around in it. The other half-hour is spent outside walking or chasing after our pups. Sheltering in place is causing me to really consider all aspects of the home we've chosen.

I remember being a little kid and realizing that each house I went into had its own smell. There was a mixture of the foods that were commonly cooked, perfumes and colognes, deodorizers, cleaning supplies, and the general habits that create the smells of the residents — things that make each family unique.

Even now, when I visit my Mom, I smell my childhood.

I'm not sure if the pandemic has changed the smell of our house, or if it's just heightened because of the increased occupancy. I do know that Adam has invested a lot of resources into buying candles, laundry beads, air fresheners, and any other masking agents he can find. He even bought a machine called an ozone blaster, but the joke is on him because no one can be in the house when you run it.

In an attempt to understand why our natural odors weren't good enough for a man who once lived in a literal fraternity house, I started looking online. When I found this, I knew I had my answer.

"The scents that you choose to surround yourself with can drive your personal behavior in positive ways," Christopher Bergland wrote in a 2015 Psychology Today article. "The scents that you surround yourself with are in the locus of your control. You can put yourself in the driver's seat, and use fragrance as a tool to create a particular mindset and increase your motivation to achieve a target behavior."

Adam likes to be in control. Not in the bad way like the toxic male characters in Lifetime movies, but in the way some normal people with a lot of responsibility look for ways to keep their environments from spinning out. And as things are increasingly spinning out of our control at work and in the world at large, it makes sense to me that he looks for ways to manage the little things that make him feel better.

To some degree, we all look for the things we can control or fix or manage. If Adam chooses to make the house smell like a mix between a vanilla cupcake, an evergreen forest, and a marina breeze, I'm all for it. And it's probably not a bad idea to make the kids shower more. Even if Ozzie's only regular activity is watching YouTube, it's not good to let all the hygiene norms fall away. We got lazy, we relaxed the rules, and we were homeschooling and working full-time, but if we're going to survive more months of being at home, we need to prioritize some semblance of hygiene.

Besides, on the few occasions that the kids get to leave the house, their level of hygiene is more important than ever. Keeping clean and vigilant about washing hands are good ways to fight the virus.

These are the little things we can do to keep everyone feeling hopeful as our Coronavirus summer drags on. The children may not be able to control if and when they will go back to school, see their friends, or get back the missed days of their youth, but we can make their home clean and inviting. When we bought the place we didn't plan on living in it this intensely, but now that we are, we can choose to keep our family scent one that doesn't give Adam nightmares, and in doing so, prosper at home.

If we don't, Adam and his array of cleaning products and air fresheners may just move into the garage.

PANDEMIC PICS

Clockwise from left: Ozzie, Ella, Mary Beth, Katie, Sadie, Adam

Adam's "super soft" 50th birthday.

Online school.

Lots of time to explore Northeast Ohio.

We actually caught a few!

The rest of the Earnheardt family: Mickey, Iggy and Jaws.

Ozzie has a bright future with DoorDash.

Lots of movies got us through the pandemic.

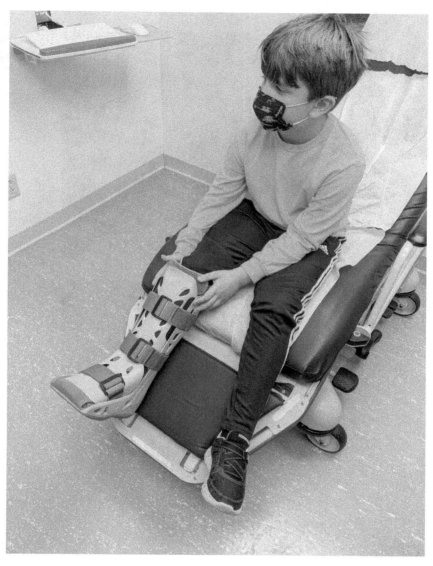

Ozzie's big break.

Getting out of the house as often as we could.

15
CREEPED OUT BY IMAGINARY FRIENDS
ADAM

Imaginary friends creep me out. No, I'm not referring to my own imaginary friends. They're fine. Thanks for asking.

I'm referring to the friends my children see, or used to see, but were never really there. At least, I don't think they were there. I'm not sure anymore. It's one of the hallmarks of childhood I've never embraced. Of course, I also never discouraged any level of imagination in my own children, no matter how disturbing.

In the early years of parenting, redirection was a useful strategy when Mary Beth and I were called on to join in on the strange and unusual play. But our kids were clever. They quickly identified our attempts to do "normal" stuff, and constantly reminded us to stay focused on their imaginative play.

When they were young, our first two children — Ella and Katie — didn't have many close friends or play dates. They relied on each other, but not until Katie was old enough to play with Ella. Because this required meaningful conversation, Ella had to wait around until Katie was 3 to really enjoy the full benefits of sisterhood friendship. Ella is 21 months older than Katie, and waiting for her little sister to be old enough to play probably seemed like an eternity to little Ella.

So, what do you do when you don't have friends or siblings around to play? You do what kids have always done. You create friends.

Sometimes these imaginary friends actually have substance. They're real, tangible objects like stuffed animals. The "others" can best be described as friends who aren't really there. They're pseudo spirits that occupy random spaces and places around our homes. When those intangible imaginary friends follow us outside the home, well, that's when things get strange. More on that in a minute.

Although there were many friends over the years, the one constant in Ella's young life was Lala. Maybe it's that I just didn't understand the need, but her constant references to Lala freaked me out from time to time. Lala was real to Ella, as real as anyone else in her life, including me.

There are countless stories of our interactions with Lala. I recall Lala joining us for family dinner, which required a separate dinner plate with actual food. Once when Ella was distracted by something her baby sister was doing, I took bites from Lala's plate. This was a bad move. Ella didn't actually see that I was eating Lala's food. Yet she turned and yelled, "Daddy! Stop eating Lala's food!"

"What makes you think I ate her food?" I asked.

"Lala told me," she said, without hesitation. How was this possible? Ella's head was turned the whole time. I'm not the stealthiest guy, but I'm sure Ella didn't see me.

"I'm sorry, Ella," I said.

"Don't apologize to me," Ella demanded. "Apologize to Lala."

"I'm sorry, Lala," I said to the empty seat, thinking to myself about the plot of this strange *Twilight Zone* episode in which I've suddenly been cast, in a supporting role no less. Let's be clear: Lala is in charge here, not me.

If you think it's strange to apologize to an empty seat, either you're not a parent or you've never been gifted with (or challenged by) a child with a deep imagination.

I'd like to say this strangeness ended with Ella. Alas, it was only amplified with Katie. In typical kid fashion, Kate mirrored the behaviors of her older sister, by developing a long and lasting friendship with Bopee. What complicated Katie's friendship for me was that, for a long time, I thought Bopee was real. Maybe she met this kid at daycare and was just mispronouncing her name? Kate spoke about Bopee with such exactness, such reflection, and such admiration that I thought for sure we'd be inviting her over for tea parties and sleep-overs. It wasn't until Bopee switched from a child to an old man that I realized it was imaginary.

This was one of many identity changes. Mostly Bopee was a kid, but it was also an elderly man, an animal, and an alien. After it became clear this was not a passing fad and we were dealing with an imaginary friend, I suggested Kate ask Bopee over for a playdate (visits from imaginary friends are awesome because you don't have to clean the bathroom). My suggestion was odd to Katie. She looked up at me with curious eyes, "Why Daddy? Bopee is here all the time."

"Huh?" I asked. "Like in your heart?"

"No, silly," she clarified. "Bopee lives with us."

Oh crap, I thought. Move over Lala, it's Bopee time.

I'd like to report that oddity stopped there. I'd like to tell you that I felt prepared for what would come next. I'd like to share that our interactions with Bopee were no more or less interesting than our dinner parties with Lala.

Instead, as if recognizing something in my realization of Bopee's position in her life, Katie ramped up the imaginary friend game to new levels. There are stories I still recall of Bopee joining us on car rides, of running into Bopee while out in public, or of trying to find space in Katie's tiny kid bed for Bopee (who apparently was larger than Katie). When I suggested once that we make Bopee its own bed, Katie said, "Only if it's in my room."

Unsure of Bopee's exact size, I suggested Katie make a place for Bopee to sleep on the floor. Big mistake. Bopee was large, and this required an even larger space on the floor. That bed space turned into a sort of shrine for Bopee where we would gather to read bedtime stories, sing lullabies and say our prayers.

No one dared disturb this space. It was Katie's physical tribute to her non-corporeal friend. If we tried to clean her room, we cleaned around the space and didn't disturb the shrine. After a year or so, when Bopee had moved on, we finally dismantled the encampment. It smelled funny.

Although it was creepy, it made me happy to see her happy. It brought me comfort to see her comforted. It also makes me think this was just the start of a burgeoning creative mind who would later turn into a gifted artist.

During COVID-19, especially in the early days, I'm sure there were many kids who, deprived of interactions with friends, required substitutions. In a few years, I'd love to read parenting research on imaginary friends to see if there was an uptick in reports in 2020 and 2021. This is because we know that cultivating active imaginations in our children is an important part of our parenting philosophy. We can't be there to participate in every activity, so we need them to create their own fun. When we can, we need to be part of their creativity and, when necessary, build shrines and tent cities to honor it.

Rather than run from the strangeness, we lean in a little more. We find new ways to encourage imagination through play and discovery. We engage by being unwitting participants in theatrical productions, dance recitals, and fashion shows. We ask questions about funky artwork and play-dough sculptures.

Bopee and Lala are gone. I miss their creepy vibe. I miss having oddball conversations with them, even if those conversations were with walls and empty dinner table seats. And while I might be missing imaginary friends, I'm thankful for the opportunity to foster that creative spark in my children. I'm thankful for their imaginative spirit, an important strength that I hope remains with them for the rest of their lives.

16

HOW I REMEMBER THE GREEK ALPHABET

ADAM

When *Mahoning Matters* founding editor Mark Sweetwood asked Mary Beth and I to pen our reflections on parenting during the pandemic, I never thought COVID would last this long. I certainly didn't think we'd still be writing this column in 2022.

Yet, like COVID, we persisted.

I'm equally surprised by my ability to recall important facts and useful tools to guide my limited understanding of COVID. These facts and tools help me navigate critical conversations with our kids about what COVID is, how the CDC and others are trying to manage it, and how we define related terms like vaccines and variants.

Remembering things these days is tough (hence my surprise). This is because I've been lost in a COVID brain fog these last few weeks. COVID brain might be a longer-term side effect of contracting the dreaded virus, but there are some things I'm proud to say, "Hey, I remember that."

As evidence, I offer exhibit Alpha: I actually remember the Greek alphabet.

I know each symbol of the Greek alphabet. I know how to spell each letter. I even know how to sing the Greek alphabet song. Much like singing the ABCs to *Twinkle, Twinkle Little Star*, there's a clever tune I learned in college. Well, in a fraternity to be precise.

Back in college, I pledged Sigma Chi fraternity. Educational requirements for becoming new brothers included learning the Greek alphabet. Our illustrious magister was brother Ron Berry. Taken from the term used to describe scholars who taught in medieval universities, the "magister" was the brother responsible for getting pledges ready for initiation.

Like other fraternities, there was lots of partying. I won't lie. That was one reason why I joined. But there was something more in the way my future brothers comported themselves. There was a very serious, reverent side to our bonds of fraternity. Note, too, that these were ideals established by a group of young men in the 1850s that we still celebrated in the 1990s. Thus, included in our preparation was a program that helped instill the ideals that served as our foundation.

At the forefront of those ideals was *The Jordan Standard,* a set of principles for guiding decisions about who could be initiated. One line in the Standard that I always loved was "A student of fair ability..."

"Heck," I remember thinking. "That's me!" I was never a straight-A student. I hated some subjects in school. But when I put my brain to it, I had a "fair ability" to pass my classes and learn the subjects I needed to get me through life. This got me through my undergraduate years until I really flourished as "a student of slightly better than fair ability..." in grad school.

We learned a lot about our fraternity and Greek life in those classes with magister Berry. But I never thought the little jingle he taught us would help decades later with COVID-related conversations. For example, when the Delta variant hit, I said to Mary Beth, "I wonder what happened to the alpha, beta, and gamma variants."

According to Louis Jacobson of *PolitiFact*, "The first four 'variants of concern'—alpha, beta, gamma, and delta—have been circulating in the United States for most of (2021). But the most dominant variant has been delta, due to its ability to spread from person to person more quickly than other variants."

Okay. Makes sense.

But last week when I was chatting with our teenage daughters about the Omicron variant, I said, "Wait. I know there are a lot of Greek letters between delta and omicron."

And then I broke out into song, *"Alpha, beta, gamma, delta..."* The horror in their eyes was delightful, the kind of look only a father of teen and pre-teen daughters can feel proud of. After all, it's a centuries-old entitlement of a father to be able to embarrass their children at a moment's notice. Fathers live for these brief moments, these rare opportunities. I mean, here I am, documenting for the world to read, prattling on about... oh. Sorry.

"Please don't do that again," they pleaded.

There are 10 letters between delta and omicron. I found it strange that the World Health Organization would just jump to omicron. Turns out, there are several "variants of concern" (alpha, beta, gamma, delta, omicron) and at least two "variants of interest"— lambda and mu—according to the WHO website. Lambda and mu were two of our missing letters.

I explained to my kids that the WHO didn't technically skip straight to omicron. It's just that the other variants didn't rise to the level of "concern." That was true for most of the letters. Another WHO report on best practices for naming infectious diseases suggested it was probably best to skip Greek letters like Nu and Xi. This was done out of concern that those letters might either confuse (Nu, when pronounced, sounds a lot like "new") or offend (Xi is a very common surname used in other parts of the world).

"Oh, my," Mary Beth said in exhaustion. "What happens when we get to Omega?"

Silence covered the room. Everyone's eyes popped in response. Because of my little ditty, they knew the last letter was omega. This was the endgame. The final symbol. Or maybe they already knew. Regardless, the thought was as ominous as the sudden hush that befell the room. It was such a weird moment that after a few moments of silence, we broke out in a few more moments of pure laughter.

I brushed it off. "Meh. I think they'll probably just move to doubling the names," I said. "Like Alpha Alpha, maybe?"

Whatever the WHO protocol, I hope we don't end up at the Sigma Chi variant someday. Having a variant with the same name as my old fraternity would just be weird.

More than anything, I hope COVID will go away forever, or at least before we actually do get to Omega. While we anticipate the end, like me, parents and caregivers of beautiful families remain, reflecting on the challenges of raising children during a pandemic, singing goofy songs about Greek letters, having a laugh when we can muster them, embarrassing our kids, and finding new ways to enjoy life along the way.

17
COVID IS NOT A GOOD TIME TO BREAK A LEG
ADAM

I walked in to find Ozzie's face soaked with tears.

It was Tuesday night. Dance night for Oz and Sadie. I found him when I came home to do the swap, dropping off Sadie and picking Oz up. He was supposed to spend the evening perfecting his hip-hop dance moves.

My immediate assumption was he was crying because of a fight with Mom, or a sister, or because someone beat him on Roblox or Minecraft.

It was worse.

Lying flat on his back, he looked up at me and couldn't catch his breath enough to tell the complete story. Mary Beth filled in the details. Apparently, after a short stint on my new exercise bike, the right foot pedal flipped back and snapped his ankle.

The extent of his injury was hard to surmise. His ankle was swollen and a little bruised, and he sure as heck couldn't dance, but it still mostly looked like he was in one piece. The thing is, I'm usually the laissez-faire-type parent when it comes to potential trips to the doctor. "Walk it off," is my typical response, but only partly in jest. There's a seldom told (but unforgettable) story of me suggesting

Ozzie had little more than a cold when he was a baby. It turned out to be something more: respiratory syncytial virus, or RSV.

He spent the week between Christmas and New Year's Eve in St. Joe's Hospital.

I never quite lived down the RSV mistake. It's not that anyone throws it in my face, it's just that — until recently — I never really learned from it either. When one of my kids has a cold, I still question the severity. "Come on, it's just a sniffle," I'd say. "You can go to school."

It's been eight years since the RSV incident and here was my son, writhing in pain, and all I could think was, "We need to get him to an ER." So, what happened, seemingly overnight, to change my worldview of childhood illness and injury?

The answer is simple: COVID-19 happened.

When the pandemic started, I recall having a nonchalant attitude toward news coming from China. Weeks later, when it hit parts of the West Coast, I simply brushed it off by saying, "Meh, it'll pass." I wasn't alone. Many didn't treat those early reports with caution or much care. As a student (and occasional professor) of gender communication, I'm reminded of studies that found men typically avoid trips to the doctors, check-ups, and mental health issues. Heck, some of us guys would avoid going to the dentist or eye doctor if it meant we could dodge a single uncomfortable interaction about our health.

In the early days of COVID, as my friends, family, and colleagues started to take it seriously, I did, too. Unlike the laggards who still refused to mask up around others, I respected the reported science and the government warnings, even if I did have some residual doubt. For disclosure: I still do have some doubts. But what's more important is that I respect the responsibility I had for the comfort of those around me.

If wearing a mask made people feel better, then I would wear a mask.

My view of healthcare was changing, even if I didn't see it. The first time I noticed this shift was when I walked in on my injured son. Any other day I would have suggested he, "walk it off", but today, I was already searching my phone for urgent care hours of operation. I even called our friendly medical doctor neighbor for advice. (Thanks, John. I owe you one. Actually, I owe you many.)

The other shift I noticed was in my temper. Before the pandemic, I might have scolded the little guy for getting on my exercise bike after countless "You're-gonna-get-hurt" warnings. And yes, he was warned, but, he's a kid. A shiny new piece of equipment appealed to him the same way freshly baked cookies do.

And it wasn't even that hard to avoid the yelling because I didn't feel angry. My normal frustration was replaced with this newfound sense of care and concern. It's not that I didn't care before, it's just that the feeling was immediate.

It might be hard to believe, but after four kids, this is our first broken bone (a point of pride Oz is pleased to brag about). We're lucky his injury didn't even rise to the level of a full-blown fiberglass cast. After a few x-rays and some follow-up consultations with the fine professionals at Akron Children's, we learned he suffered an avulsion fracture. This is where a small chunk of bone attached to his ligament was pulled away from the main part of the bone.

Yeah, ouch.

When I was required to use crutches as a kid, I hated them. Ozzie loves them and treats them like a badge of honor. And here's the funny part: he doesn't really need them. The ER doctor prescribed them as a precaution until we could follow up with the pediatric orthopedic specialist. The specialist said he doesn't need the crutches. We learned that the boot is more than enough to stabilize the ankle while it heals (that was a big relief for Mom who ensures the children take occasional showers).

Ozzie was there to hear the news, that crutches were not required, and we've repeatedly said, "Hey dude, you don't need those." But he doesn't care. He likes the attention that comes along with injury. He uses it to guilt his sisters into playing Minecraft with him and to command attention from his friends at school. Not only does he wear a cool mask, but he also has a boot and crutches.

It's hard being a dad. I feel pressure to provide for my family, to make sure bills are paid, that homework is done, the kitchen is clean, and that home repair projects are (kind of) done. I feel pressure to make sure everyone is "OK." Sometimes the pressure of trying to keep everyone safe makes me frustrated. Sometimes I even feel a little taken for granted.

But I also know this will pass. My hope is that when the pandemic is done and things go back to normal, I'll remember how good it felt to let go of the anger and lean into the caregiving.

18

WHEN COVID REACHED THE EARNHEARDTS

ADAM

There's a line in the Netflix series *House of Cards* that's my favorite of the series.

It's not much. Just two words at the end of season 5's last episode. They're powerful and slightly "out of character" for the character who says them.

After supporting his evil schemes and being a player in his story for years, Claire Underwood ignores a phone call from her disgraced husband, former U.S. President Frank Underwood. Breaking the fourth wall, Claire looks up to the camera, speaking directly to the audience, and says, "My turn."

As most critics (and fans) can attest, the next season of *Cards* was arguably the worst. So, my thought right now is, "Does this mean that, like season 6 of *Cards*, my attempt at writing about parenting during COVID will suck?"

I hoped not.

And, to be honest, I didn't have a lot of time to worry about how my writing would stack up to Mary Beth's. This is because, as I write this, I'm *much more* concerned about something *much more* important.

. . .

One of our kids tested positive for COVID.

Yes. It finally happened. After almost a year of bobbing and weaving, masking and purifying, isolating and quarantining, the COVID-19 plague reached our door.

Call it fatigue from dealing with doctor visits and Google searches and quarantine confusion and rapid tests and arguments, but Mary Beth just didn't want to write about our kid getting COVID. Not right now. Probably not ever. I don't blame her. This was hard.

Still, we both agreed on one thing: documenting family life during the pandemic would be incomplete, and most certainly insincere if we avoided sharing our first COVID-KID challenge.

What happened exactly, you might ask? Who got it? When? How? Well, obviously we know some of those questions can never be answered. We can only speculate on the how and when. But who? One of the girls tested positive in mid-January. Thankfully, for her, COVID-19 manifested as little more than a bad head cold. In fact, we were so sure it was her normal allergies that we didn't even realize she was actually sick until the "normal" medicinal options failed us.

I didn't want to take her to the doctor, but Mary Beth felt differently. So, our daughter was tested on a Friday, which meant waiting the weekend for the results.

I took the call from the pediatrician's office on Monday. "You're kidding, right?", I asked.

Mary Beth could hear the *Please God, no* plea in my voice as the nurse on the other end reaffirmed the test results. "Yeah, but how accurate are these tests, really?" I asked. "Shouldn't we get her retested? I hear a lot about false positives."

"They're the ones we send out," the nurse said. "They're the most accurate."

Getting the news was bad, but also completely on-brand for the pandemic.

First, the child who contracted COVID-19 had been bebopping around the house for two days straight. Friday, she was sick. Saturday and Sunday, she was ready to rock. Now it was Monday and she felt fine. She wanted to return to school, but we kept her home. Any symptom of the virus was long gone. No cough. No sniffles. No droopy eyelids.

Second, it was the start of the return to a four-day school week. The kids had been back to a post-holiday 2-day-a-week, in-person schedule. The children were excited to go back and looking forward to some normalcy. But suddenly being placed in quarantine the day they were supposed to feel "normal" again was a blow to everyone's psyche.

Third, we've learned the hard way that the length of quarantine when you're the primary caregiver for a COVID-19-positive child is longer than the currently recommended 10- to 14-day isolation period. Protocols for who should quarantine and when and for how long vary from place to place. Rules for returning to school and work were hard to manage and left us feeling confused.

We're 11 months into this thing. You'd think we would have answered the who, where, why, and for how long questions by now.

So, to deal with all these changes and challenges, we turned inward for support. I mean, aside from an occasional DoorDash delivery and curbside grocery pick-up, where else were we going to get support? We've relied on family from day one. Why should day 346 be any different (and yeah, I actually kind of counted the days)?

While the kids still had online school, and Mary Beth and I worked from a distance, we found ourselves returning to the things that helped us through the early days of the pandemic: puzzles, games, playing with the dogs, the Nintendo Switch, cleaning the house, and working on projects that we suddenly had the time to complete.

What I realized over the last few weeks is that we would be terrible on our own. Writing a solo column is one thing, but living quarantined under the same roof surrounded by people who love us (and put up with us) certainly made isolation a lot less lonely.

19
REDISCOVERING RIDICULOUS(NESS) ROUTINES
ADAM

Like many '80s kids, I often complained about one of the biggest disappointments of my youth: MTV.

"What happened to MTV?" we would ask, albeit rhetorically. We knew what was happening, we just didn't know why. Now when we mention MTV to fellow Gen Xers, it's become more of a punchline than a grievance.

For those of you who don't know, by the late-90s, the first-ever, full-on music television channel was morphing into something barely recognizable from its origins. Music videos went away only to be replaced with reality tv and variety shows. The only music videos on MTV these days come from the short clips played during their annual awards show.

Music fans had to say goodbye to the music. Gone were our favorite artists. Gone were our favorite MTV VJs like Martha Quinn (my teenage crush), Nina Blackwood, J.J. Jackson, and Adam Curry. Gone were MTV News updates via Kurt Loder. These days it's refreshing to see old VJs show up in new places, like Matt Pinfield in an odd music documentary (he's a walking music encyclopedia), or

Carson Daly on a morning show. Even Alternative Nation VJ Kennedy has her own talk show on, of all places, the Fox Business Channel.

The format change led to the extinction of all MTV VJs. Search Wikipedia for a list of MTV VJs and you'll find "past" VJs by channel. Turns out MTV had a lot of channels. But for obvious reasons, the "current" MTV VJ list is blank — obviously, because why would you need a VJ if you no longer play music videos? Okay, no more rhetorical questions. I promise.

I watched a lot of MTV in the 80s. Probably too much. Watching MTV was part of my after-school routine, even if it was just on in the background while I was doing homework. My sister and I often watched until the wee hours. I watched with my friend, David Lovic, because, as he liked to point out, it was "educational." How else were we going to become the next U2 if we didn't consume their videos as often as we could?

There was something extra comforting in this routine. Seeing my old "friends" like Duran Duran, Talking Heads, Janet Jackson, Madonna, and Tom Petty — names now synonymous with some of the most classic music videos — energized and inspired me.

Over the last decade, I would occasionally stumble upon an MTV show and get sucked in by a "Teen Mom" or "16 And Pregnant" storyline. But when I realized I was watching this play out on MTV, I would quickly reject it out of protest, or maybe it was fear — as if my eyes would somehow melt away from seeing the ruins of music television (yes, that's an Indiana Jones, Lost Ark homage; again, '80s kid).

This was true until, during the pandemic, Ozzie and I discovered "Ridiculousness."

If you're unfamiliar with the show, it's a lot like "America's Funniest Home Videos," with the exception of one important rule. See, AFV viewers are encouraged to submit their own silly videos. "Ridiculousness" forbids this, in part because they don't want to be held liable for injuries some people clearly receive in these clips.

In truth, I knew about "Ridiculousness" long before Ozzie and I started watching. It was one of the few shows on MTV I could tolerate for more than 2 minutes. Sure, "Jackass" — another former MTV staple — was fun and certainly entertaining. But there was something pure and unadulterated about listening to host Rob Dyrdek banter with his longtime co-hosts Sterling "Steelo" Brim and Chanel West Coast about the "ridiculous" videos they found and cleverly edited together into related categories.

Plus, there was a short, albeit slightly irrelevant Ohio history lesson to teach Ozzie while watching "Ridiculousness." First, Dyrdek, who gained fame as one of the world's greatest skateboarders, is an Ohio native (Kettering). Second, the theme song is based on Devo's hit "Uncontrollable Urge." Devo (another great '80s band) hails from Akron.

Like the MTV of my youth, watching "Ridiculousness" marathons with Ozzie has become a sort of morning ritual during the pandemic. We record a bunch of episodes (it's not hard, MTV programs the show for several hours nearly every day) and then fast-forward through the commercials and some of the banter (especially when a guest is on the show). I'm also careful to fast-forward through some of the more R-rated clips, the stuff that's a bit too inappropriate for my little guy's eyes. We like to get to the good stuff — the videos.

When we watch, we laugh. We laugh hard. In fact, we often rewind to rewatch the clips that made us laugh the hardest. I know it sounds wrong to laugh at someone else's pain. I'm careful to explain to Ozzie that these people are "OK" and that aside from an unlikely trip to a doctor's office, they'll probably walk it off and feel okay. "Like twisting an ankle," I explain. "You walk it off and forget about it."

While writing this column, we're watching Season 10, Episode 23. The category "Player Slayers" is a collection of videos of people being rudely interrupted while playing video games. Each gamer is focused on the screen in front of them, headsets on so as to block out all other distractions in the room, about to slay a dragon or beat a game when — BOOM! — someone kicks a ball in the gamers face, smashes an egg on their head, or pulls a power cord.

This particular category is extra funny today because, as Ozzie notes, "Oh man, this one hits a little too close to home. I'm just glad it's someone else and not me."

We stop. We rewind. We watch again. We pause. We laugh, sometimes harder than the first time. There's something deeply cathartic about watching someone land the wrong way on a railing (often on their crotch) or face plant into the carpet while performing a risky living room maneuver. I explain to Ozzie that while it's wrong to laugh at someone else's pain, to remember that, well, they also recorded this and uploaded it for the world to see.

Maybe they want us to laugh along with them. Or maybe not. Maybe I'm just a horrible parent. We'll know soon enough.

All I know right now is that the routine of waking up, loading up a recording of our new favorite show, and laughing together is more important now than it ever was. The pandemic has given us more time to spend together (maybe too much), and I can't think of a better way to spend it than laughing with my son. I've come to understand that the MTV of my youth will never come back. Music videos drop on YouTube and Vimeo now and that's okay. I can even find my old favorites. Now I can load up Duran Duran's *Hungry Like the Wolf* and watch whenever I want. But I've made my peace with this because MTV has come to mean something different now.

Similar to how I used to watch music videos with my friends, I now watch funny videos with my family. It's part of what we're calling the "new normal" that speaks to my evolution. Introducing my kids to musical acts via MTV and music videos is harder to do now, and that's OK. Because just like classic '80s music videos, a perfectly timed crotch shot or header into a ceiling fan or an out-of-control dance move at a wedding reception will never go out of fashion.

Those kinds of videos are capable of bringing us all great joy when we need it most.

20

GONE FISHIN'
ADAM

I started fishing when I was a kid. It's hard to calculate the importance this activity had on my childhood, particularly in regard to my mental well-being.

When I was a boy, my family wasn't exactly what an outsider would call stable. Don't get me wrong, my parents loved me and worked like dogs to provide the best life they could. Their work was complicated by a host of challenges. They were very young and very poor when I was born. My sister was born 16 months later. As we grew, my mother would often regale us with stories of our little family sleeping on a mattress on the floor of a small apartment near Killeen, Texas — with small rodents and large spiders loitering nearby.

Although my parents carried large reserves of love for us, their other, more basic resources were limited. Around the time I turned 7, my dad started having very serious mental health issues. So, it was also about this time that I had to grow up and become responsible in the ways most little boys shouldn't have to.

When my dad was hospitalized, I was the "little big man" of the house — "little" because, well, I was 7, and "big" because I was much too tall for my young age. I was often confused for someone much older and mature. Of course, young people pushed into a position of responsibility realize quickly that older and mature are not the same thing.

But, in the midst of unpleasantness, arguments, uncertainty, breakdowns, police visits, and ambulance trips, my mom always tried to find ways for me to remember I was still a little boy. As much as my extended family enjoyed crowning me "man of the house," my mother found ways to protect what little innocence remained.

One of her methods for reminding me I was a kid was to send me out with Uncle John. My uncle was a true outdoorsman and he loved to take me fishing. I still remember the excitement of waiting for him to pull up and take me to Potter County in Pennsylvania for a long weekend of trout fishing, or closer jaunts, catfishing on Locks 8 and 9 of the mighty Allegheny. We'd stand in the creeks and on river banks for hours, just being in the moment and enjoying nature, trying rather unsuccessfully on most days to catch fish.

When the pandemic hit, I suddenly found myself with oodles of unexpected extra time. I tend to be a workaholic. Someone who likes to spend hours accomplishing professional goals quickly realizes that working all day can be exhausting in ways that cause physical and mental harm.

But in true workaholic form, when I was grinding, I didn't notice the exhaustion. This was true until the early days of the pandemic. Routines were interrupted and lockdowns made all my work homebound, which is not the ideal location for pursuing (let alone accomplishing) professional goals.

Being cooped up in the house wasn't good for me, Mary Beth, or the kids. My natural state is restlessness and that quickly became an irritant to everyone, including me.

I like to be productive, and COVID only heightened my Mr. Fix It and Mr. Clean ambitions. Look, it's just really hard for me to sit on the couch and watch Netflix for hours on end. I wake up and move. When my head hits the pillow, I'm out (and I sleep hard).

One day last April, I was in the garage looking for something to fix when I saw my old fishing gear. It hit me like a bolt of lightning. I would fix myself in the same way my mother tried to fix me. I would escape into nature, just like I did when I was her little man. I would find quiet, peace, and fresh air — the tried-and-true ingredients for resting my mind, body, and spirit.

No masks are required when you're sitting on the edge of a lake or standing in a favorite trout stream. The only "six feet" you think about might have to do with the depth of the water in a favorite fishing hole after an evening of light rain, or the distance you hope your next cast will go to reach the spot where you just saw a "big one" jump.

Who cares about social distancing when there's no one around for miles?

Because I associate fishing with some of the best times of my childhood, it's probably not surprising that I love to take my kids fishing. If you've ever fished with little kids, you know how challenging that can be. You learn quickly that taking your own fishing gear is pointless. When you fish with kids, there is no time for your own angling. You're too busy baiting hooks with "ewww, gross, squiggly, slimy, please don't hurt him" worms.

And, if you ever manage to get a worm on the hook, you're quickly called in to untangle a cast from a nearby branch. Even if the line makes it in the water, it's bound to get stuck on some damn log floating near the bottom that's close enough to see, but too damn far to unsnag. Which starts the process over from the beginning.

And don't get me started on what happens when one of my kids hooks a bluegill.

As much as I love giving myself carpal tunnel from tying endless knots, I decided to leave the kids at home this time. If I was going to reconnect to my childhood love of fishing, I was going by myself.

As a workaholic and father of four, alone time wasn't something I previously explored. I want to experience the world with my kids, so I feel guilty about leaving them behind. I worry my kids might miss an opportunity to experience something unique about life if I don't bring them along.

But after months of being locked together in the house, it was fairly easy to push away the guilt and download some fishing apps. I scoured Google results for the best fishing in Pennsylvania and Ohio and set out for adventure and relaxation.

It took me a while to get back into the swing of things. My hip waders had dry rot (not easy to replace when you're six-foot-eight. Some tackle was rusted. Worst of all, my body wasn't as flexible as I remembered. How did I ever climb up and down slippery river banks?

But after a few months, I was fully back into the swing of things. I managed to get out on the first day of trout season this year in Pennsylvania. It was one of the most restorative acts I've taken in my adult life. Being a tech guy who is lost without a smartphone, I had become disconnected from the natural world. Reconnecting to it was just what I needed to breathe again. Really breathe.

Like many of you, I've lost a lot during the pandemic. It's been difficult. It has changed me. But, when I stand in Chest Creek near Mahaffey, Pa. and cast my line into the cool, clear waters, I know that I've reclaimed something I lost long ago, something that was always important, always central to my mental health.

I've found the healing power of nature and the spirit of a little boy who took solace in the company of fish.

Now I just need to remember how to actually catch one.

21

WHY I (PROBABLY, REALLY) STARTED PLAYING FORTNITE AT 51

ADAM

Most men in their 50s are not gamers. At least not the guys I know. We 50-somethings don't even look like gamers. We're not even close to the image one conjures when asked to picture a gamer.

Instead, mention "gamer" and an image of a prepubescent with eyeballs fixed on a screen, holding a controller or a mouse in one hand while the other clicks away at a keyboard, head adorned with earphones and mic, surrounded by empty pop cans, chip bags, chocolate bars, and candy wrappers.

It looks bad. It looks slothful. Of course, we now know it's anything but lazy. For gamers, it's a real sport, maybe even an art form. In most cases, it's positively a social environment for kids. They're in it for fun. Some are playing for glory, clout, and even cash.

But that's not me. I suck at these games. I don't win much. When I do, it's a sad display of contorted dance moves meant to serve as gloating the likes my wife hasn't seen since I played beer league soft-ball. What's even sadder is that the only ones there to see it are my wife and 9-year-old son. They laughed at first. Now they just look at me with pity.

So then, "How did I end up here?" you might ask. At 51, why have I been playing *Fortnite* every day for the last two months? Yes, I know I don't resemble the typical gamer. Most people won't think of an overweight, bald, out-of-shape, Gen Xer, with a voice as deep as Leonard Cohen's, going toe-to-toe with some stripling gamer halfway around the world.

Plus, whoever that little kid is, she or he usually kicks my ass.

No. I'm most definitely not in it for glory or cash.

The path to my gamerdom probably doesn't seem all that unusual. Still, my motivations don't align with that of a traditional gamer. This is because I started playing to connect with my son. And, if I'm being completely honest, I started playing because it looked like fun.

Quite frankly, it's a weird environment for someone my age. I didn't know this going into my recent gaming foray, but I'm absolutely, positively the oddball on *Fortnite*. Yes, there are a lot of kids in this game. A lot. It's rated T for Teens, but I get the sense there are more kids my son's age than actual "teens" playing this game. According to *Dot Esports*, the "T" rating simply means the game is appropriate for players 13 years old and older, and that parents of younger kids should consider this when allowing them to play the game.

This is exactly what we did as the parents of a 9-year-old obsessive Fortniter. We had (and still have) long talks with Ozzie about gameplay, who is playing, and about making smart choices when interacting with others in the game.

Still, therein lies a big problem for the gamer guy in his 50s. There are options for playing the game with a headset and microphone because you can team up with other players. Playing *Fortnite* in squads (groups of four) is a popular option among young gamers. You're expected to communicate with these other players. Of course, they all sound like my son and not Johnny Cash. So I can't very well drop my deep, bassy Dad voice into the open chat.

Sorry. I know creepy when I hear it. That's a strange boundary I won't cross.

When my 9-year-old son started playing, he was motivated by his connection to his friends. It was a way to hang out after school. I lurked over his shoulder, convinced that some weirdo would try to friend him. If I heard a voice like mine on the other end, I'd have questions. Lots of questions. So I can't (I won't) play *Fortnite* like the rest of them unless they suddenly come up with a special "over 30" league for us old-timers.

Yes, I just called you 30-somethings "old-timers" (at least I didn't call you "Boom..." oh, never mind).

But when Ozzie played, that didn't happen. No stranger danger, at least not yet. I know his friends and they know Dad isn't only looking on, he's playing. Although I'm sure there are weirdo predators out there who mean to do harm to kids like my son, this looked like a safe enough environment, in part because I was part of it — even if it was a bit strange when my son's friends started to send me friend requests.

I politely declined, by the way (or maybe I ignored them; I don't remember).

Looking on with concerned parent eyes while Ozzie played, I got hooked. There was an ease with which I adapted to the gameplay, which was very important for someone who doesn't have the same fine psychomotor skills as a 9-year-old. This is important because I'm an old guy who finds escape in a kids' game. Some people my age have other hobbies to release and unwind after a particularly stressful or busy day. Maybe it's exercise or a good book. Maybe it's TV or music. Maybe it's a long hike through Mill Creek Park.

My stress reliever — at least, right now — just happens to be a game I downloaded to the Nintendo Switch. (Fun side note: it's actually my Nintendo Switch, a 50th birthday present from my kids because I was always stealing their Switch to play *The Legend of Zelda: Breath of the Wild*. But I digress.) It's been good for me, for my mental health, for my connection to my son.

In fact, playing *Fortnite* has had two very positive outcomes.

First, my son feels more connected to me. My daughters are *Fortnite* haters. They hate everything associated with the game and think it's quite hilarious that Dad is now a Fortniter. Now Ozzie has someone at home who cares about *Fortnite* almost as much as he does. He is wrapped up in the lore of *Fortnite*, the stories that surround the game. Before my interest, he only had his friends to share those stories with. Now he has me, and I love to hear that little voice share his views of the world with me (even the virtual ones).

Apparently, I'm late to the party because there are many stories of past chapters and seasons I've missed. He feels like he's teaching me important facts, even though I know those stories won't really help me play the game.

He's pretty darn good at it, both playing the game *and* in the telling of *Fortnite* lore. He wants me to learn all the characters and their histories and repeat them back to him. He quizzes me from time to time, and I'm proud to say, I'm starting to pick it up (even if it does nothing to help me earn a victory crown in a solo match).

This storytelling is the best part of how he and I share in the experience. We went to a YSU basketball game, and he spent the entire first half telling me about *Fortnite*, clearly uninterested in the awesome game that was being played right in front of him. But he had my undivided attention, and that was more important than a few slam dunks and a YSU win.

The second outcome is a little harder to describe but equally important to my mental health.

I get excited when I win in *Fortnite*. My blood pumps a little faster when I take a victory crown or level up after finishing an important quest. As inconsequential as it sounds (and trust me, I know how it sounds), I feel like I've accomplished something.

People my age tend to become more nostalgic as we get older, looking back on lives fulfilled personally and professionally, reviewing timelines for triumphant moments, and scanning for pictures of our past that make us reminisce, smile and cry. We do this because we want to rekindle feelings of youth, maybe grasping at faded memories of sitting in front of a large TV screen playing *Mike Tyson's Punch-Out!!* on the original Nintendo or maybe *Pac-Man* on an Atari 2600 console or *Pong*.

It doesn't matter what the games are, because what really matters is that playing them makes me feel like a kid again. When I play, I feel a little immature, in a good way, if even for a few minutes. When I play games and the virtual world gets a little intense, I like the feeling of euphoric stress, like watching the ending of a close sports game or the climax of a scary movie — a good kind of stress that excites the senses.

Sure. I started playing *Fortnite* because it was a fun, exciting way to reconnect to my childhood. Maybe even to unwind a little. But the fact that I can play as a way to connect with my kid is hands-down the only victory crown, clout, or quest reward I'll ever need.

22

LEARNING TO REALLY DRIVE. AGAIN.

ADAM

Sharing a house with four kids is, in many ways, a wonderful experience. There's always something happening. There's always laughter and play. There's an occasional tear accompanied by an opportunity to swoop in and play hero dad. There are communal meals where we catch up on each other's lives. There's always someone you can talk into watching a movie or playing a video game with you.

It's a blessing to be surrounded by people.

The flip side to the joy of being surrounded by "these" people is the frustration of never being alone. When we're all home, I am often reminded that I'm responsible for the well-being of others. There's an appointment here, a lesson there, a forgotten item for school, a drop-off at a friend's home. There are endless "to-do" and "honey-do" and "been-meaning-to-fix-that" lists that are often jumbled together in a quantum conundrum that only a particle physicist could untangle.

Okay, maybe it's not that complicated. But forget being alone. Sometimes I just want to be with my wife in the same space with no one else around. Yes, of course we share a bedroom. But when our heads hit the pillows these days, we're out for the count. No time to check-in, to catch-up, to chit-chat. It's turn on Comedy Central, hope for a rerun of South Park, and be out before Cartman says something horribly inappropriate.

Before the pandemic, Mary Beth and I managed to find moments of escape when the kids were at school and on play dates. During the lockdown, these kid-free moments mostly disappeared.

So, like most couples stuck sheltering in place with their kids, we coped. Instead of going out to lunch when the kids were at school, we hit the road. We loaded a cooler and went for a drive with no particular destination in mind. We took to the back roads of northeast Ohio and western Pennsylvania.

Our car became my new favorite hangout. What might have been a midlife crisis brought on by a global pandemic was mitigated by a road trip revival.

Spending time behind the wheel came naturally to me. For many years, I was on the road doing admissions work for the University of Pittsburgh and later, Clarion University of Pennsylvania. I logged thousands of miles from the Midwest through New England. I had a routine. There were favorite websites for downloading maps (MapQuest, anyone?), but mostly I didn't care if I got lost. It was part of the adventure. There were recurring thoughts of "Wow, no one really knows where I am right now."

Being alone on the road was as freeing as one would expect, but it also came with a sense of power. When I got out of admissions and got married, my wife and I traveled I-80 twice a week for 3 years while we studied at Kent State. These were great drives full of conversations about a shared future, building a family and negotiations, infrequent arguments, and occasional debates about ideas we'd covered in class.

We finally moved to Liberty Township, a suburb of Youngstown, Ohio, in part because it's only a few miles from work. This move put the brakes on our extended road trips. The time we spent together in the car was less important, replaced by the mundanity of life.

When COVID hit, I found the open road again, reminded of what it's like to feel free and alive. What I didn't realize is that my pandemic-prompted rediscovery of driving bliss would also coincide with my oldest daughter's 16th birthday. She's now old enough to get her permit, and with it, the first glorious moments of teenage freedom.

Convincing Ella that these glorious moments are within her reach has been tougher than I expected. While most kids would relish the opportunity to get behind the wheel and escape their parents and siblings by cruising Belmont Avenue or Market Street, Ella is less inclined.

She wants freedom, but she's also apprehensive about the responsibilities (and perhaps reluctant to become an Uber driver for the family). Most days I can appreciate her hesitant nature. Helicopter parents would probably love a kid like Ella because the thought of their little baby cruising the streets in a 2-ton machine would not mesh well with their overprotective psyches.

Not me. I'm not a helicopter or lawnmower or whatever-they're-calling-it-these-days parent. I want her to go. I want her to explore. I want her to get that learner's permit, and eventually a license, and explore the world - just so long as she remembers to pick up milk and be home by 9 p.m. (8 p.m. on school nights).

Because of Ella's reluctance, I've been making the case for driving. Reminding her that she likes to be alone, to be in her head, to think about life and the world around her is my modus operandi. "What better place to do this than in a car?" I say, only half-convincingly, I think. I tell her to picture what it would be like to turn up the tunes, roll down the window, and go on a mini-adventure. I tell her that driving can free her brain from the complexities of life, and that it's a great way to unwind.

I appeal to her growing sense of independence. Ella has threatened to "walk" to the Dollar Store with her sister, Katie. I used this request to remind her that a car would let the two of them go to exotic locales such as Mill Creek Park and the Eastwood Mall. My desire to convince Ella to drive isn't completely unselfish. I dream about kicking Ella and her siblings out of the house for a few hours so Mary Beth and I can talk, or watch a movie, without constant interruption. I think about sending Ella to pick up her sister from dance when I'm just too damn tired to move.

More importantly, I want Ella to just drive, to just get lost - not on the roads, but in the moment of being alone with the kind of freedom only an official state-issued driver's license can bring. For any of this to happen, Ella needs to take the driver's test. Yesterday, when I noticed Ella was "in her head" and thinking about life, I took it as an opportunity (once again) to push the test.

"Why not study this weekend and take it next week?" I asked.

She said, "Yes." It took every ounce of energy to contain the gigantic smile and "Sweet!" welling up inside.

I'm not dumb. I know that a surefire way for any parent to dissuade a teenager from anything is to look happy or be enthusiastic about it.

I played it cool because I want this for Ella. I want my baby to experience the joy you only find by taking on challenges and succeeding. Driving is her next milestone. Just as I watched my baby girl take her first steps or say her first word, I want to be by her side when she flashes her beautiful smile for the folks at the Ohio BMV. I'm willing to take the hit to our insurance premium to make it so.

23
CELEBRATING A FRIEND'S 50TH BIRTHDAY
ADAM

Last week, my good friend and colleague, Jaietta Jackson, turned 50.

Now, I am a gentleman who would not normally out the age of a woman in the local news. But these are special circumstances. In the case of Jai, I'm sharing because she basically celebrated her birthday for an entire month. In doing so, she took her friends on an uplifting journey in the middle of a really crappy time.

When I got the "save the date" in late-May, it struck me that there was something more than a little taboo about it. A birthday party? Like a real, honest-to-goodness, drinks and food and other goodies? For adults?

After all, we've been living under lockdown for nearly 18 months now. Businesses closed. Weddings and graduations were postponed. No retirement celebrations. Loved ones who passed were buried without proper funerals. Up until a few months ago, I'd grown accustomed to living in a COVID world where parties were a strict no-no. Now, here's my buddy Jai offering the forbidden fruit (for what it's worth, Jai had candy-covered apples for goodies).

As I thought about it, I started to sense what others were feeling:

that under the right circumstances, celebrations are a must for our sense of psychological well-being, for cultivating connections with friends, and for letting loose.

We are allowed to do things like this again. For now, anyway.

But then I started to worry that I just wouldn't remember how. How to act like a (fun) adult. How to tell fun stories and connect with old friends and make new ones. How to dance (yes, "dance").

Don't get me wrong. I spent a good deal of my youth partying. I was in college for many (many) years. The 1990s were a good time to be a young man. I'm an extrovert who gains energy from being around people, and so I was very, umm, "energetic" in my 20s. As a matter of fact, one of the biggest problems for me during the pandemic was finding a way to cope with a lack of social interaction. Now I had a chance to socialize and celebrate the life of a good friend, and I was a little intimidated by the opportunity.

The party was a lot of fun. There was dancing and amazing food and a signature drink called "Jai's Fabulous 50 Rum Punch" (I have no idea what all was in it, but it came via a bartender who poured it from a magical jug). I saw friends from work and people from the community and we all laughed and talked and enjoyed each other. We also enjoyed the long-forgotten taste of freedom. We enjoyed feeling like unencumbered adults at play.

It wasn't until Mary Beth and I were back at home that it hit me. I didn't just have a good time. I was nourished by the celebration. It felt like having a large drink of water after working in the yard all day. It was satisfying to feel alive again.

I get that many people don't often enjoy social situations the same way I do. Many have commented to me how freeing it felt to be locked down during COVID and the comfort they get from isolation. But I think that's exactly what Jaietta's party did for me. In my case, however, I found comfort in being freed from the lockdown. And I think her party came just at the right time.

Now we're seeing new lockdowns and mandates because of the Delta variant. While vaccines appear to do a good job of preventing serious illness from this more contagious strain, I'm worried this could be a setback.

I haven't given up on Fall, but it's hard to not lose a bit of hope when our march "back to normal" takes a left turn down a dead-end alley. When the vaccines first came out, I pushed aside any doubts and got it as quickly as I could register. I got the shot for many reasons, but perhaps the most compelling one was my kids.

Just like Jai, I turned 50 during the pandemic. By comparison, my 50th birthday in October 2020 was much quieter than Jai's. And like many of you, I've struggled since March 2020 with navigating the "do's and don'ts" of COVID. Still, for the most part, I don't feel like I'm missing out on much. This is but a brief blip in my life.

I've made a lot of memories and gained a lot of youthful experience, but it's a different story for my kids and their friends. My 8-year-old has spent about 50% of his life wearing a mask in public (his calculations, not mine; we're working on his math skills). My 11-year-old gets to hang out with her friends on Google hangouts and not sleepovers. My 14-year-old is transitioning into her high school years with trepidation about quarantines. And my newly minted sweet 16-year-old hung out with her family on her milestone birthday this past weekend instead of having a big party with her classmates.

We got closer to normal, but we're not there yet.

If part of growing up is learning to manage expectations and delay gratifications, I predict that the pandemic kids will be especially good at this. I'm a heel for promising them that things are going to be better soon. Maybe I should have said, "sooner than later." My tone is still always upbeat and hopeful when I remind them to pull up their masks and maintain a little extra distance when around other people.

I'd be lying if I didn't admit that my hope is starting to wane. I keep telling them that we're going to have a mask-burning party. I no longer give a "save the date" for that party.

It's my own fault for feeling this way. I allow myself to hope that we're close to the end. When my YSU students are feeling down because they've been spending "the best years of their lives" in Zoom meetings instead of Penguin tailgates and house parties, I'm the one who tells them that we'll be back to being happy on campus "sooner than later."

In my lifetime, I've used hope to bring me through a lot of dark moments. It's a powerful psychological force that humans need to survive tough times.

As Dale Archer puts it in his *Psychology Today* article, "Hope is the belief that circumstances will get better. It's not a wish for things to get better — it's the actual belief, the knowledge that things will get better, no matter how big or small. It's the belief that at age 55, after a disaster where you've lost your home, car, and possessions — everything material, that you still have your health and family, and that you can and you will start over."

Seeing Jaietta celebrate with the full force of her 50 years gave me hope when I needed it the most. Now I'm trying to share that hope with others. COVID isn't sticking to a timeline, but with every celebration, I'm reminded that someday I'll be partying with even more friends on a regular basis.

Partying will be sweeter this time around because I'll remember how hard life is without it.

24

I'M A LOSER, BABY

ADAM

Like many families, ours is a quirky mix of interests, temperaments, talents, and convictions. This is evidenced by the debates in which we engage, many of which pit Mom and Dad's amazing Generation X against the kids' Generation Z.

Mostly, we enjoy these debates because they allow our Gen Z kids to explore the impact of ideas in the context of something bigger.

To be clear, I used the term "impact" in the previous sentence for a reason. You see, our little Gen Z army would kindly request we refer to it as "influence." They're wrong, of course (as usual). Gen Zers only think they influence other cultures because of memes. They are largely credited with turning "OK, Boomer" into one of the most often used stinging meme-insults of the last few years.

Yeah. Real clever. Reminds me of "Thanks, Obama" or "Let's Go Brandon."

Then, just as quickly as the insult hit mainstream and became uncool, they abandoned it and moved on to things more obscure and kitsch.

This type of rapid-fire interest/disinterest is typical, but having

Gen X parents might hit harder for Gen Zers. The kids are mostly disinterested in Mom and Dad because Gen X is generally a throw-away in the world of memes. Our generation is famous for being ignored. Those who care about generations prefer to examine the impact of large and powerful Boomer and Millennial cohorts. This is because most Boomers and Millennials don't mind open engagement in cultural warfare.

Among Gen Zers, however, it's almost as if ignoring Gen X has become a kind of unspoken meme in itself.

"Gen X? Meh. Never heard of it." I can envision a Gen Z kid saying this, followed by "You look like a Boomer."

We do our best to represent Gen X affinity, but the act of being proud of these sorts of distinctions doesn't come naturally for the 80s and 90s kids.

Unlike us, our little Zoomers take great pride in the way they're turning out. The differences can be exhausting, but the COVID slow-down has given me the opportunity to develop a better under-standing (dare I say, appreciation?) of Gen Z.

So, in my humble opinion, I posit that Gen Z might just be alright.

Here's why.

During a long car ride, Mary Beth and I reminisced about popular songs from our youth. This is, at times, a challenge for Mary Beth because she's not a big music lover like me. But pick a really big hit from the late-80s or early-90s, and she can wax poetically about a boy or a party or some other significant moment in her life where that song and, most importantly, its lyrics influenced her life.

Our conversation turned to Beck's 1994 hit, "Loser." The lyrics are strange, but we talked about the series of images in the music video (which was in wide rotation on MTV back then). It reminded us of today's Gen Z meme culture.

"Loser" strikes a chord with me as much now as it did in '94. It's interesting, complicated, artistic, and totally weird. Like totally, man. Totally Gen X. And, we thought, maybe totally Gen Z?

So, after our chat, I tried a strategy that parents have used for dozens of years: I asked the kids to listen to my music.

I wish I could say they got it. I wish I could say the kids sang in unison, "I'm a loser baby." I wish I could say they asked us to play it over and over again and gushed about the cultural relevance of a song from 40 years ago. It would be a better story to have a strong moment of generational understanding, an overlap of fields of experience, and a deep connection to our Gen X past.

That's not quite how it went down. They listened out of obligation. Maybe they thought, "If we listen, Dad will buy us ice cream." No. When the song ended, they peppered us with requests for their music. And, like any good parent, I turned the control (via my phone and Spotify app) to them while Mary Beth and I died inside.

Gen Z music is bad. Really bad. Unoriginal and mostly retreads of music we loved in the 80s anyway (lots of synth in Gen Z tunes). It mostly consists of YouTubers and artists and gamers who string lyrics together with weird jingles that sound more like a music bed for a Skittles commercial than anything in Casey Kasem's *American Top 40*.

In some cases, it's worse. Much worse. They've ripped off songs from our past and replaced the lyrics with their own nonsense.

They call them parodies. I call them parasites.

I had found the perfect crossover Gen X/Gen Z song. I mean, what Gen Zer wouldn't love these lyrics? To those who don't understand Beck's references, they sound nonsensical:

You can't write if you can't relate
Trade the cash for the beef for the body for the hate
And my time is a piece of wax falling on a termite
That's choking on the splinters.

But when I saw their happy faces in the rearview mirror, I decided to dig deep into my Gen X soul and react in a way the grownups in my life rarely did: I leaned in, but not initially in a Sheryl Sandberg "lean in" kind of way. I literally leaned my old man ears into the speakers to try to discern the lyrics among the poppy top-40-wannabe beats and chords.

Then I found myself really leaning in, physically and mentally. I got over my initial disappointment and started listening to appreciate. I didn't want to be the irrelevant old person who can't learn from a new generation, and instead, I chose to open up and tried to appreciate Gen Z music.

It wasn't so much what I heard that led to my "a-ha" moment.

It was the realization that their songs are just as important to them as mine were (and still are) to me. Just like the late-80s and early-90s music scored the soundtrack of my youth, Gen Z is at the stage of life where music is important. It's different and just not as good as mine. And that's okay.

In fact, according to Ajay Kalia on *Skynet & Ebert*, we're most susceptible to new music in our teens through our early 20s because there are a lot of changes happening in our brains. I was 24 when Beck's "Loser" hit the radio and MTV. That might seem old by musical influence standards, but Kalia also argues that our brains don't typically stop discovering new music until our mid-30s.

And, well, we started having kids when I was 35.

But maybe the fact that I still fondly recall a song that was a hit when I was 24 gives me hope for my kids who are just now discovering music that will serve as memory triggers for them later in life.

Our oldest is 16. Our youngest is 9. I estimate this gives me nearly 10 to 15 years or so to influence the soundtracks of their lives. Maybe, just maybe, if I pick the right songs and do it just right, someday they'll pull up an ancient Spotify road trip playlist I made for them and influence their own kids with mixtape masterpieces of the totally, radically greatest generation: Gen X.

In that case, nothing would make me happier than three generations of Earnheardt losers, baby.

25

MY 'SAVE FERRIS' MOMENT

ADAM

My 'Save Ferris' moment came courtesy of Stan Boney, an award-winning anchor for WKBN News in Youngstown, Ohio.

If you're unfamiliar with the reference – 'Save Ferris' –you probably haven't watched *Ferris Bueller's Day Off*. Or maybe you have and just don't remember. I mean, it's been a while since it debuted.

For me, it's the quintessential 80s teen comedy chock full of memorable scenes.

From Bueller's lip-syncing parade performances of Wayne Newton's *Danke Schoen* and The Beatles' *Twist and Shout* to principal Ed Rooney's fight to bring the school-skipping Bueller to justice, to Ben Stein's brief performance as a monotone economics teacher – 35 years later and I still hear references to those iconic scenes.

By far, one of my favorite shticks is the escalation of Bueller's fake illness–his reason for missing school. He has nearly everyone fooled. It's called the 'Save Ferris' moment. His unassuming schoolmates wrongly assume Bueller is dying of some terrible disease (although no one knows what it is) and thus embark on a campaign to save his life.

"Umm, he's sick. My best friend's sister's boyfriend's brother's girlfriend heard from this guy who knows this kid who's going with this girl who saw Ferris pass out at 31 Flavors last night," says a random classmate to the teacher taking attendance. "I guess it's pretty serious."

Bueller masterfully invented this moment, a simple reason for skipping school that has grown out of control. He could care less. "It's pretty tough coming up with new illnesses," he explains. "It's pretty childish, but so is high school."

The 'Save Ferris' concept worked so well that it weaved its way into our popular lexicon. For example, a moderately successful ska band from the 90s adopted 'Save Ferris' as their moniker (check out their cover of Dexys Midnight Runners *Come on Eileen*). It spawned a tourism debate about whether or not to reprint 'Save Ferris' on the same water tower from the film. You can even buy a 'Save Ferris' t-shirt on Amazon.

I thought about *Bueller's* 'Save Ferris' moment a lot when Boney called me. Unlike Ferris, I was really sick. But like the gag, I felt silly, maybe even a little embarrassed, for even getting sick in the first place.

Why feel embarrassed for getting sick?

Like some Americans, I traveled to celebrate Thanksgiving with friends and family. Like some Americans, I returned home with COVID. Now, I'm not the type to make assumptions about when and where, and how I contracted it. But those particular pieces of information were only important for contact tracing (which I did).

I was angry and probably a little irrational, too. "So much for being fully vaccinated," I often lamented.

The week following Thanksgiving was the worst. Anyone who's fought a non-hospitalized bout with COVID will tell you that the fevers, chills, congestion, sore throat, and breathing difficulties, in the beginning, drain every ounce of energy. Not that the hospitalized version is any better. It's just that when you're isolated, it feels like the rest of the world could give a crap less.

You're not in the hospital. You're not going to die. Suck it up and get better.

See. Just a little irrational.

In those first few days, I wasn't 100-percent sure I actually had COVID. The official test results didn't come until a few days later. By then I was convinced I had it based on one very specific symptom: the loss of smell. When showering with some particularly strong-smelling body wash, it hit me, "Umm, I can't smell this. Uh oh."

A week later, I probably still wasn't up for taking work calls, but I didn't care. I was sick of being sick. I wanted to feel normal. I looked like crap, and I sounded worse. Stan called and we talked about something completely unrelated to COVID. He could hear it in my voice. "Are you okay? You sound sick," he asked.

"Yeah. I'm still dealing with COVID."

"Oh no. Feel better man," he replied. I don't know Stan that well, but I know him well enough to know he was concerned. Of course, I wasn't that sick at this point. At least not nearly as sick as the week before. A full week-plus into COVID and I had turned a corner. I was beginning to wonder if I even really knew how to be sick anymore. Like really sick. Do any of us know how to be sick anymore, or has COVID messed that up, too?

About an hour later, Stan texted: *Can I interview you about getting COVID? We've gotten away from telling the stories about people who have it.*

I hesitated, but he texted me again two hours later with the same request.

I texted back: *Sounds good. Heads up: I don't look real great. LOL!*

When it aired, the story was about me getting COVID. *Ugh, so what,* I thought. I'm not even that sick. My wife and kids watched and teased me for the next few days about it, in part because of my reaction. I could handle the ribbing from my family, but I didn't know how to deal with what came next. Texts, emails, and social media posts started rolling in from friends and colleagues.

"Are you okay?"

"Do you need anything?"

"This is like that 'Save Ferris' thing," I told my wife. "And Bueller was 100-percent faking it." I reminded her about the scene, and that I was embarrassed by the outpouring of support.

"Why not just be sick and accept the get-well-wishes for what they are," she said. "Just be sick and let people take care of you, and care about you."

She was right. I should have remembered how to be sick, receive messages of care from friends, accept advice and offers of support, and spend time healing and resting.

See, COVID has tricked us into thinking, "Meh, it's just a cold." We can go to work and school and parties and live our lives each year with colds. The reaction I received from friends and the advice I got from my wife and others taught me that I need to remember how to be sick. I need to stay in bed, stay hydrated, check my temperature and pulse oxygen levels, and let others care for me.

And, yes, I need to spend considerably more time on self-care.

Of course, Stan's story wasn't about me. It was never meant to be, even if that's how it was framed (and how my family and I viewed it). It was more about the uptick in COVID cases Stan and others were seeing.

"Within just a few hours today I heard of three people I knew with COVID," he texted me later that day. His concern was valid, of course, and he saw a need to use my case to bring attention to the surge.

Still, would I have been flattered if my social media friends and readers of *Mahoning Matters* suddenly launched a "Save Adam" campaign? Of course! In all seriousness, the only person who could save Adam at that moment was Adam. And that's what I did. I'm feeling better, and even if it feels strange and unusual, I'm going to lean into self-care and take a little more time for myself.

My first step? Getting my hands on a 1961 Ferrari 250 GT California for a joy ride around the streets of Youngstown. Top down. Mask off.

26

WAS COVID-19 OUR COLLECTIVE MIDLIFE CRISIS?
ADAM

I think I'm in the midst of a midlife crisis.

Of course, I'm not a psychiatrist, but my behavior and attitude in the last 18 months seem to match the profile of someone in a crisis.

There's no real APA or DSM-V psychological definition of someone in a midlife crisis, but there is for someone in an emotional crisis. According to the American Psychological Association, someone in crisis demonstrates a "clear and abrupt change in behavior."

Someone in emotional crisis might show a:

- Neglect of personal hygiene
- Dramatic change in sleep habits (e.g., sleeping more often, not sleeping well)
- Weight gain or loss
- Decline in performance at work or school
- Pronounced change in mood (e.g., irritability, anger, anxiety, or sadness)
- Withdrawal from routine activities and relationships

For sure, I can click 3, maybe 4 on that list (OK, not the first one; I'm still pretty good about wearing deodorant, brushing and flossing, taking showers, etc.). But I worry about poor sleep habits, being overweight, and my occasional crappy moods.

Of course, I'm blaming this midlife crisis on the pandemic.

If you're like me, no matter where you are in the world, your life was upended in some form or fashion by COVID. The early days led many of us to hunker down. Fellow extroverts, longing for social fuel, lamented being cut off from supply lines found in the usual spaces like bars and churches. Those who lived by regimented schedules saw an end to normalcy, forced to recreate routines in hopes of retaining control of their calendars.

To be fair, we're all living through the same midlife crisis. Look at the list above again. How many can you check on a daily basis?

I'm lucky in some ways. I'm lucky to be surrounded by family, even if it didn't slow my descent into another midlife crisis. Yes, another. That's the rub. This, I think, is my second midlife crisis. Without knowing much about how to define a crisis, I ignorantly assumed we could only have one.

Recently, I likened my current midlife crises to taking a test in college. Like a college exam, there can be more than one in a particular semester. They can come at any time. Some come without warning.

If you're familiar with how college calendars work, think of your life in terms of a semester. You come to the first class on the first day, unsure about the expectations. As you move through the term, listening to lectures and reading, you learn more and more until at the end of the semester, the final class comes, possibly with an exam. Then, it's over.

It's the final. It's the culmination of the work completed in one semester.

Did you pass the final exam? Who knows? That's not really the point (at least not for my midlife-midterm metaphor). It has more to do with what you learned, how you grew, and how you managed the multiple (yes, multiple) midterm tests you took along the way.

My amazing wife is also a professor. She's taught me many things about teaching: how to create testable learning objectives, building fun course materials, and how to manage a classroom. She also taught me something about midterm exams that blew my mind: there can be more than one.

Never, ever did I have a professor who gave more than one midterm exam. Or so I thought.

"Sure they did. They just didn't call it a midterm exam," Mary Beth explained. "But you certainly had professors who gave you more than one test in a semester, right?"

"Yes."

"Boom. Multiple midterm exams," she replied. "Just because it happens in the beginning of the semester, or the middle, or near the end, doesn't matter. It's all midterm until you're in finals week."

I know. Either she's brilliant, or I'm not as smart as I think I am, or I'm really overthinking this whole thing.

This is why I believe, regardless of age, we're all experiencing some form of a pandemic-induced midlife crisis. If my "life in a semester" metaphor holds true, our crisis "exams" can come at any time. So, to paraphrase Mary Beth, it's all midlife until you're in your final moments.

See, I had wrongly assumed that 1) I'd only ever have one midlife crisis and 2) it would actually come at midlife. According to Amy Morin, psychotherapist and editor-in-chief at *Verywell Mind*, midlife crises can come at any time. But people generally assume they come somewhere between their 30s and 50s.

"People who are having a midlife crisis are thought to be struggling with their own mortality, and, somewhere during midlife, they ditch some of their responsibilities in favor of fun."

My first crisis came sometime in 2014. Sure, I struggled some with my own mortality, but that wasn't really it. I just wanted to break free of my responsibilities and have more fun. "I'm 44," I thought. "This means it's time to have a midlife crisis. I can deal with this."

Plus, in a strange way, the thought of living to be 88 was comforting.

Our collective COVID midlife crisis may have forced many of us to consider our own mortalities. But I think it really forced many of us to reconsider the importance of life, in terms of fun, in terms of seizing the moment.

"Carpe diem, boys. Seize the day." Those lines, famously whispered by Robin Williams as John Keating in *Dead Poets Society* are words that resonate with many of us today and we look to emerge from our crises by seizing the day. Mary Beth wrote about seizing the day during COVID in an earlier chapter.

While COVID sent some of us spiraling inward, it also sent some of us out to seek out fun, to escape, and to be curious about life. According to psychologists, this is also a typical reaction to a midlife crisis. "The emotional turmoil some people experience during midlife doesn't always lead to major lifestyle changes that involve the desire to be young again," Morin notes. "In fact, a midlife crisis could turn into something positive."

See, midlife crises don't have to be all bad. They can produce something meaningful. My first midlife crisis helped me realize the importance of my identity as a father and husband. My second midlife crisis made me reconsider the importance of exploration and experiencing new things with my family.

If there's a third midlife crisis in my future, I'm ready for it. I'd just prefer it not be brought on by a global pandemic.

EPILOGUE
ADAM & MARY BETH

We didn't start writing columns about being a family in a pandemic with an end-date in mind. We never assumed it would last two years either. We wrote columns every week, then every two weeks, then only when the mood hit us, or when we felt we had something relevant to say. Then, as restrictions lifted and life came back to a new normal, we ended our writing stint with *Mahoning Matters*.

Still, as we continue to emerge from COVID's lingering effects, we continue to grapple with that question: "How much longer?"

If you haven't guessed already, we heard that question often during our countless trips up and down I-80, crossing the border from Ohio into Pennsylvania and back, road trips to our decommissioned family church-turned-cabin. We spent a lot of time and money rehabbing the old church into a sort of pandemic family refuge, an escape of sorts. Apparently, this was the thing to do during the pandemic – clean, paint a room, install new drapes, clean, declutter, clean some more, fix up an old church. There were some projects we took on, including the church rehab, that often begged the question: "How much longer" until this is done.

Most parents and caregivers who have taken children on any car ride longer than 5 minutes know that question well. If it's not "How much longer," it's "Are we there yet?" We suppose any variation would have been a good title for this book. But there was something special about "How much longer" that resonated with us in a way that others did not. Maybe it's because when we heard "How much longer," it was quickly followed by phrases like "I'm bored" and "I'm hungry" and "I have to pee."

Whether we were deep in the Pennsylvania Wilds or hunkered down at home in Youngstown, we heard the question in its many forms: How much longer until we get to camp? How much longer until the pizza gets here? How much longer before the iPad is done charging? How much longer will we be teaching online? How much longer is this stupid Zoom meeting? How much longer will I need to wash these damn masks?

How much longer until COVID is over?

It was in these moments, often prompted by these questions, that we gave thanks for being a family. This made the question of "How much longer" was easy to answer, even if it wasn't the answer we were all looking for. The answer usually took the form of "I don't know, but..." followed by "...at least we have the Internet," or "...at least we have DoorDash," or "Netflix," or "the (Nintendo) Switch."

Our favorite answer was, "I don't know, but at least we're together." They weren't the answers the kids wanted, but they helped us to focus on our blessings.

It was in these moments that we took stock of what really matters—being the best version of a family we could be when life was at its worst, living in the moment, rather than asking how much longer.

ACKNOWLEDGMENTS

Thanks to the amazing editors who have reviewed our work over the years, including *Mahoning Matters* editors Mark Sweetwood and Justin Dennis, who provided us endless support and praise during our tenure as columnists for their fine publication. If you're interested in news about Northeast Ohio, we encourage you visit their site. Do a quick Google Search and you'll find them.

Next, we met Michaela Fosdick via Fiverr. She served as copy editor for the publication you see here. Michaela found the little things we missed. And there were a lot of little things. If you're in the market for a great copy editor (at an incredibly reasonable rate), search for mfosdick94 on Fiverr and give her some work.

Finally, and most importantly, we acknowledge the work of our children. They are gifted and talented, which would seem like something most parents would say about their kids, except that we have proof. Some of that evidence can be found in the pages of this book, but we get to see their brilliance play out every day in everything they do. They're kind, loving souls we are eager to share with the rest of the world. And what the world certainly needs more of are kind, loving souls. Our little "Team EKSO" would make any Mom and Dad proud parents.

ABOUT THE AUTHORS

Dr. Adam C. Earnheardt is a professor of communication and general education coordinator at Youngstown State University. He has written several books on sports fandom and communication. Adam served as executive director for several organizations, including the Youngstown Press Club and the Ohio Communication Association, and as interim executive director with the National Society of Newspaper Columnists. His column writing focuses on the intersections of parenting, sports, social media and technologies.

Dr. Mary Beth Earnheardt is a professor of journalism and former director of the Anderson Program in Journalism at Youngstown State University where she serves as advisor to *The Jambar*, the school's student newspaper, and other student media. She previously served as president of the Society for Collegiate Journalists and also served as the Society's executive director for several years. Mary Beth is the author of *Switch-A-Wish* and shared weekly column writing duties with Adam for *Mahoning Matters* during the COVID-19 pandemic.

Adam and Mary Beth reside in Youngstown, Ohio with their four children - Ella, Katie, Sadie, and Ozzie, two dogs - Iggy and Mickey, and a cool cat - Jaws.

CPSIA information can be obtained
at www.ICGtesting.com
Printed in the USA
LVHW031429220323
742294LV00013B/758

9 780997 955118